S0-BBS-332

A Place to Cook

Inspiring cookery courses
around the world

Jenni Muir

A Place to Cook

Inspiring cookery courses
around the world

For David

Published in 2004 by Conran Octopus Limited
a part of Octopus Publishing Group
2–4 Heron Quays, London E14 4JP
www.conran-octopus.co.uk

Text copyright © 2004 Jenni Muir
Book design and layout copyright
© 2004 Conran Octopus Limited

All rights reserved. No part of this book may
be reproduced, stored in a retrieval system,
or transmitted, in any form or by any means,
electronic, electrostatic, magnetic tape, mechanical,
photocopying, recording or otherwise, without the
prior permission in writing of the Publisher.

The right of Jenni Muir to be identified as the Author
of this Work has been asserted by her in accordance
with the Copyright, Designs and Patents Act 1988

British Library Cataloguing-in-Publication Data.
A catalogue record for this book is available from
the British Library

ISBN 1 84091 392 4

Publishing Director: Lorraine Dickey
Senior Editor: Katey Day
Assistant Editor: Sybella Marlow
Art Director: Chi Lam
Designer: Victoria Burley
Picture Research Manager: Liz Boyd
Picture Research: Clare Limpus
Production Manager: Angela Couchman

Printed in China

Contents

Introduction

There are some unfortunate souls who still see cooking as a chore. However, this book is for people who love it, and love it so much that they will enthusiastically devote their hard-earned holiday time and weekends to pursuing their passion.

Studying food is a great way to travel. It's more fun than queuing up with the backpackers and weary coach passengers at the main tourist attractions. Of course you get to eat a lot better than tourists normally do at motorway service stations, familiar chain restaurants and homogeneous hotel dining rooms. But perhaps most important is that it is a marvellous way to meet local people, appreciate their way of life and share a common interest.

Cooking holidays, leisure courses and gastronomic tours are now big business. In addition to the sophisticated gastronauts always seeking new taste sensations and ways to expand their repertoire, there are many people who love good food but realise they have limited skills when it comes to producing it at home. They revel in the opportunity to learn, and the relaxed conviviality of a leisure-based cooking course offers an unintimidating environment in which to practice and improve.

The growth of interest in this area unfortunately means that many businesses are seeking to exploit the market rather than cater to it. To ensure you get value for your money, there are several points you must consider before enrolling on a course. What attracts you to this one in particular? If it is fronted by a celebrity chef or food writer, check to see whether they will actually be teaching the classes; often they don't. Celebrity chefs can be disappointing demonstrators and lousy teachers, and you may well be better off with one of their trusted staff or colleagues, but consider the cost of the course in this context. Do not kid yourself that you are paying to rub shoulders with the culinary elite when they may not even be on the premises.

A famous name may seem like a guarantee of reliability, but there are many excellent courses run by people of whom you will not have heard too. And sadly, plenty of others that should not be offered at all. When considering a course, investigate what expertise the company has in this field. Naturally, they need to know what they are talking about, but they also need to be good communicators and charming, professional hosts. If it is a residential course, what will be the standard of accommodation and service? You do not want to waste your precious time or money helping to pay off someone's imprudent purchase of a romantic property in Tuscany or Provence. Check out the background of the owners and teachers, and seek advice from other enthusiasts and authoritative independent consultants before booking.

Not everyone has the time, job or lifestyle that allows them to devote a fortnight to a culinary holiday, no matter how inspiring the programme. Be aware that even a week-long course can take much longer once you factor in travel to a foreign country and transfers from the airport. It's disappointing, too, when the course is only offered once or twice a year, on dates that don't suit you.

I didn't want you to open this book and find 25 luscious courses you could not attend. For this reason it features a variety of different types of class at various price points: some of just a few hours suitable for enjoying on a weekend or quick stopover, others with luxurious accommodation, restaurant visits and trips to wineries and artisan food producers included. I've also favoured companies that have a dynamic year-round programme, or courses that run at least four times a year. An increasing number offer tailor-made classes, where the timing and subject matter can be built around your interests and requirements. Obviously this can command a price premium but in our time-poor society such flexibility is attractive and desirable. Do however check the minimum number of participants required — irritatingly some companies assume you happily travel with several other adults in tow.

I hope you enjoy visiting these courses as much as I have.

Jenni Muir

Tony Tan's Unlimited Cuisine
Melbourne, Australia

Born in Malaysia, his mother a professional cook renowned for her English butter cakes, his father a restaurateur, Tony Tan railed against the idea of becoming an accountant and instead followed the career that was in his heart and his blood. He trained in the restaurant kitchens of Melbourne and at leading schools in Europe, became a successful chef and restaurateur, but now prefers to spend much of his time teaching. Esteemed Australian chef Stephanie Alexander describes his cooking as 'savoury, masterly and absolutely mouthwatering'. With his broad experience of food and culinary techniques from around the globe, there can be few people better placed to lead classes in the exciting spheres of pan-Asian and modern fusion cooking.

Tony Tan rolls an old wooden spoon along the side of his kitchen workbench. Obediently, the tuile biscuit pastry curls neatly around the handle to form a perfect cigar-shaped scroll. 'See? People assume this is hard but it's really very easy and requires only the most basic equipment,' he says. 'I've used nothing but a wooden spoon handle to turn this regular tuile into *a gorgeous* tuile. There really is no need to go overboard buying specialist tools.'

He starts turning out his coconut custards ready to serve. 'Whoops! See how soft this is? The custard should wobble.' He nudges it towards the centre of the plate with the help of the plastic ramekin. 'In Singapore coconut custard is like a rock, but this is very much lighter, light enough that it can be enjoyed at the end of a dinner by people who love desserts but don't want more than a little. And it's essentially nothing but a crème caramel made with very special ingredients.'

Indeed, this dessert is even easier than the traditional French one because there's no need to caramelize sugar and use it to line the inside of the moulds. Instead Tony simply drizzles a bottle of dark, treacly kitul palm syrup from Sri Lanka over the plated custards. 'Before the palm blossoms, the sap is tapped, then boiled to produce this syrup,' Tony explains.

He finishes the dish with cubes of fresh, seasonal mango. 'I like to take advantage of whatever is in the marketplace. Mango is at its optimum right now and is ideal for the wonderful, tropical, summery theme of this dessert.'

Tony has been cooking since he was a child growing up in Malaysia. 'My dad was a restaurateur while my mum did the cooking. We also had a head chef called Heong Sok who refused to let me near the woks. These three people influenced my perception of food and fuelled my passion for cooking. They were constantly talking about flavours, textures and quality of ingredients.'

He moved to Australia in 1976 to finish university. 'My dad wanted me to study accounting but I chose to fail so I could

OFTEN DESCRIBED AS EUROPEAN IN STYLE, MELBOURNE IS CONSIDERED AUSTRALIA'S MOST SOPHISTICATED CITY.

ABOVE: THE TIAN OF TUNA INCORPORATES PRETTY LAYERS OF SALMON ROE AND CUCUMBER, WHICH MAKES A SAVVY DINNER PARTY DISH, IT IS MUCH EASIER TO MAKE THAN IT LOOKS.

OPPOSITE: TONY WORKS HIS CULINARY MAGIC.

work in restaurant kitchens. From these beginnings I bought Shakahari Restaurant in Melbourne, then opened Tatler's Café in Sydney. It was only in the 1980s that I decided to return to university to complete my degree in Renaissance History and Chinese Language.'

He was on his way to a Masters degree when a call from renowned Australian chef Stephanie Alexander persuaded him to cook a series of regional Asian curries to match fine wines at her restaurant. This shot him back to national prominence in the culinary world.

In 1995 Tony was asked to teach at various cooking schools, colleges and festivals in Australia and abroad, and he's been doing the same ever since. 'The main reason I

started teaching is that I have always been a firm believer in imparting knowledge to anyone who really enjoys food and culture. I love interacting with like-minded people. I also believe in taking amateurs and professionals by the hand and giving them the tools — that is the best techniques, the best ingredients, the best imagination — to achieve excellence.'

Tony is as much at home in the Italian cafés, butchers and delicatessens of Melbourne's Lygon Street area as he is in the Oriental groceries and bakeries on Victoria Street in Richmond. Warmly greeted at every shop and restaurant he walks into, he regularly conducts market tours, most frequently helping to decipher the fascinating products sold on the strip

Tian of Tuna with Salmon Roe and Cucumber

Lemon myrtle is an Australian bush ingredient that can be purchased from some specialist food stores. If you can't find it, Tony recommends substituting 1 teaspoon of finely grated fresh kaffir lime peel, or leaving it out altogether. You can use king fish in place of tuna, if desired. Be sure to deseed the chilli to keep its flavour subtle.

SERVES 4

1 tomato

1 small cucumber, about 10 cm (4 inches) long

1–2 spring onions (scallions)

160 g (5½ oz) bluefin or sushi-grade tuna, finely diced

120 g (4¼ oz) avocado, diced

4 teaspoons chives, finely chopped

2 teaspoons fish sauce

1 teaspoon deseeded and minced fresh red cayenne or Dutch chilli

1 fresh kaffir lime leaf, finely shredded. (alternatively use the tender new leaves of lime, lemon or grapefruit)

½ teaspoon dried, ground lemon myrtle

a pinch of sugar

4 heaped teaspoons salmon roe

salt and freshly ground white pepper

a few black sesame seeds, lightly toasted

FOR THE VINAIGRETTE

1 teaspoon sushi rice vinegar

1 teaspoon sherry vinegar

½ teaspoon sugar

80 ml (3 fl oz) (⅓ cup) grapeseed oil, or other light vegetable oil

a dash of light soy sauce

salt and pepper

Put a kettle of water on to boil. Use a serrated knife to score a small cross in the base of the tomato, then place in a heatproof bowl. Pour the hot water from the kettle over the tomato and leave for about 1 minute. Drain, then slip off the skin. Quarter the tomato, use a teaspoon to remove the seeds, then finely dice the remaining flesh. You want about 3 tablespoons of diced tomato. Set aside.

Peel the cucumber then, using the vegetable peeler, cut the flesh into thin ribbons. In a small mixing bowl, whisk together the ingredients for the vinaigrette, then add the cucumber ribbons and set aside for 10 minutes.

Cut the spring onions into fine julienne strips, enough to give 2½ tablespoons. Set aside to use as a garnish.

In a medium-sized mixing bowl, combine the tuna, avocado, chives, fish sauce, chilli, kaffir lime leaf and lemon myrtle. Add the sugar and a little salt and freshly ground white pepper. Gently stir, being careful not to over-mix, or the dish will be mushy.

Put a 5 cm (2 inch) diameter stainless steel or PVC ring on a serving plate. Half-fill the ring with the tuna mixture and cover with 1 heaped teaspoon of salmon roe. Remove the ring carefully. Repeat with the remaining tuna mixture and roe to give 4 servings. Arrange the cucumber ribbons around the tian, garnish with the spring onion julienne and toasted black sesame seeds, and serve.

MALAYSIAN FEAST, ASIAN SALADS, SASSY SHANGHAI AND MODERN THAI ARE AMONGST THE CLASSES ON OFFER.

known as 'Little Saigon'. However he can also guide visitors around Melbourne's superlative Queen Victoria Street market and the smaller but sophisticated market in trendy Prahran, which houses one of the country's best cookware stores.

People naturally come to Tony for authoritative classes in the secrets of Nonya cooking, modern Chinese fare, authentic Balinese and anything to do with spices and noodles. However, he is 'hopelessly infatuated' with Spain, having spent several years visiting the country. In Melbourne, he is renowned as an accomplished vegetarian chef too.

The published schedule includes intimate evening demonstrations starting with champagne and concluding with a relaxed,

convivial dinner. Saturday classes tend to be hands-on workshops starting at 10 or 11 am and finishing around 3 pm.

First-rate wines carefully matched to each day's menu are supplied by the prestigious Australian company Brown Brothers, whose wine educator Steve Kline also works alongside Tony to present food- and wine-matching masterclasses. Throughout the year, interesting guest chefs are showcased to provide new stimulus to regular attendees. Recipes for Tony's own classes are changed regularly, to keep the teacher as well as his students fresh and enthusiastic. 'I guess this is in keeping with my philosophy of learning, of pursuing excellence, and keeping up with trends in Asia and Europe,' he explains.

In addition, Tony gives private tailor-made courses for professionals. He is particularly sought-after by chefs looking to achieve a better grasp of modern Asian and fusion styles, of which the tian of tuna (page 11) is an excellent example. In this he skillfully combines ingredients from Asia, the Mediterranean and the Australian bush in a dish that is both simple to make and easy to serve.

Expect to find professional as well as amateur cooks signing up for Tony's two-week culinary tours to destinations such as China, Thailand and his beloved Spain, 'now my second home'. These are fastidiously plotted to ensure that guests experience the highest standard of teaching each destination has to offer and, of course, the most memorable cuisine.

Courses currently available

Evening classes including:
Sichuan Hot & Spicy – a popular course, featuring Chinese regional dishes with flavours ranging from hot, pungent and fragrant to the beautifully subtle. A vast range of other classes are offered. No accommodation included.
Singapore Style – this class covers different types of Singaporean food featuring 5–6 recipes that are easy to replicate.

Half-day courses including:
Spice Box Workshop – Cooking with spices exploring the range of fresh Asian herbs and dried spices and how to use them.
Market Walk – a tour around Victoria Street with advice on the bewildering choice of fresh herbs, spices, cuts of meat and unusual seafood.

Contact: Unlimited Cuisine Company
28a Lansell Road
Toorak
Melbourne
Victoria 3142
Tel +61 (0)3 9827 7347
Fax +61 (0)3 9826 4977
www.tonytan.com.au

Sydney Seafood School
Sydney, Australia

Sydney's fish market is the largest of its kind in the southern hemisphere, auctioning around 55 tonnes of seafood and more than 100 species from around the globe each day. It is an important commercial business centre but, unlike other working markets in the world's major cities, is situated in the heart of the metropolitan area and welcomes the local general public as well as tourists. The fish market's purpose-built teaching facility is designed to educate amateur and professional cooks as well as trade buyers in all aspects of seafood cookery and handling. In particular the school aims to promote the wide variety of seafood available, giving people the skills, knowledge and confidence to cook with new and different species — so important in today's climate of over-fishing and threatened extinction of popular varieties.

The slogan is 'where the city meets the sea', and if you want to get acquainted with seafood there can be few places better than the cooking school operated by Sydney Fish Market. Authoritative in its subject, yet — like the city itself — enthusiastically incorporating the latest culinary trends and developments in aquaculture, it attracts professional and amateur cooks from around the city, around the country and around the world.

The programme, which runs throughout the year, features a range of courses based on particular species (for example, dealing with oysters), cooking techniques (such as barbecuing seafood), favourite cuisines (Chinese, Spanish), and classes devoted to popular dishes, such as stir-fried chilli crab, bouillabaisse and paella. Australia's leading chefs, including Tetsuya from Sydney and Cheong Liew from Adelaide, make frequent appearances. When 'prodigal sons' such as chefs David Thompson and Christine Manfield, both of whom have forged successful restaurant

careers overseas, return to visit Australia, they are joyously welcomed back to the Seafood School to teach.

Each class begins with a demonstration in the well-fitted 66-seat theatre, then progresses to the next-door teaching kitchen. Here participants work in groups of six to prepare the dish they have just witnessed. A jolly seafood meal with wine follows. On weekends the format is expanded from two hours to four and, in the case of classes based on Oriental and Southeast Asian cuisines, may begin with a visit to Sydney's Chinatown to identify and purchase authentic ingredients. However, it is the seafood barbecue course that is by far the most popular and, even in this nation of experienced outdoor cooks, is offered several times a year and always attracts a waiting list.

Damien Wright, head chef of the Manly Wharf Hotel, made his demonstrating debut at the fish market with a dish of barbecued baby barramundi, gremolata

THE FISH MARKET IS IN THE HEART OF SYDNEY AND, WITH ITS OWN TRAIN STATION, IS EASY TO ACCESS.

Barbecued Barramundi with Gremolata and Potato, Asparagus and Rocket Salad

SERVES 6

FOR THE GREMOLATA

- 100 g (3½ oz) sourdough bread, crusts removed
- 150 ml (scant ⅔ cup) extra-virgin olive oil
- 80 ml (3 fl oz) (⅓ cup) vegetable oil
- 2 lemons, peeled and roughly chopped
- 2 garlic cloves
- 2–3 bunches flat leaf parsley
- 2–3 tablespoons capers

FOR THE SALAD

- 1.5 kg (3 lb) Kipfler, Ratte or Fingerling potatoes
- 24 spears green asparagus
- 300 g (10 oz) rocket (arugula)
- 6 shallots, sliced
- juice of 2 lemons
- 100 ml (3½ fl oz) (scant ½ cup) extra-virgin olive oil, plus extra for oiling vegetables
- salt and white pepper

- 3 whole lemons
- 6 whole baby barramundi, about 500–550 g (1 lb–1 lb 2 oz)
- salt and freshly ground black pepper
- a little vegetable oil, for brushing
- a little olive oil, for brushing

Damien Wright's dish 'takes just 15 minutes, as long as you're organized'. By this he means boiling the potatoes and whizzing up the gremolata sauce in advance. If you can't get baby barramundi, use similar-sized whole fish from the snapper family, or salmon, but not thin fillets of white fish as they will break up too readily on the grill plate. The gremolata can also be served with scallops or lamb.

To make the gremolata, roughly chop the sourdough bread and place it in the bowl of a food processor. Drizzle the bread with the extra-virgin olive oil and leave to soak for 5 minutes.

Meanwhile, begin the salad. Place the potatoes in a large saucepan of water. Bring to a boil and simmer until the potatoes are just tender. Drain and set aside to cool.

Finish the gremolata by adding the vegetable oil, chopped lemons, garlic, parsley and capers to the food processor. Blend to a coarse purée, then transfer to a serving bowl and set aside until ready to serve. Cover and chill if desired.

Heat a ridged grill pan, char-grill or barbecue. Peel the cooked potatoes, then cut them into even slices. Trim the asparagus. Lightly oil the potato slices and asparagus spears, then cook until browned on both sides.

Meanwhile, in a large mixing bowl, combine the rocket, shallots, lemon juice and extra-virgin olive oil. When the potato slices and asparagus are cooked, add them to the salad, mix gently and set aside.

Take the 3 whole lemons and cut about 2.5 cm (1 inch) from each pointed end, then cut the remaining centre pieces into thick slices. Place them on the grill with the widest sides facing down, press down gently to release the juice, and cook on one side only until the cut surface has caramelized to a golden brown. Set aside.

Use scissors to remove all the fins from the fish. Wash the fish and pat dry. Use a knife to score them three times evenly across each side. Lightly season with salt and pepper, then brush with a little vegetable oil or olive oil, or both.

Lay the fish on the grill and cook for 5–10 minutes on each side until done. Meanwhile, loosen the gremolata with a little extra oil to make it pourable or spoonable as desired.

Arrange the salad on serving plates, then add the cooked fish, a dollop of gremolata and a slice or two of grilled lemon per person.

sauce and salad. It's typical of modern Australian food in that it draws inspiration from Mediterranean cuisine, but applies it to Australian ingredients and lifestyle.

'Barbecuing is definitely the way we're going at work,' he tells the class. 'It's a very light, healthy way of cooking and everyone seems to love it. If you're using a fire barbecue rather than a ridged grill pan or electric grill plate, you need to start it a good 20 to 30 minutes before you want to cook the fish, so that the flames have a chance to die down and the coals are glowing. When the grill is smoking hot, wipe it with a wet cloth. This helps prevent sticking and removes any excess oil or carbon.'

Barramundi has for many years been Australia's most esteemed fish and is native to the coastal and fresh waters of the tropical northern half of the continent. The name is an Aboriginal word meaning 'river fish with large scales'. In the wild, this species can reach up to 1.5 m (5 ft) in length and 50 kg (105 lbs) in weight, though most of the fish caught these days weigh less than 6 kg (13¼ lb).

Baby barramundi, which are fairly new on the market, are an interesting choice. Sometimes called 'plate-sized', they are farmed commercially in sea water and have a light fresh flavour. Although the older, larger barramundi caught in rivers are more expensive, they can, by

comparison, taste muddy. Damien advises choosing a baby fish no smaller than 500 g (1 lb) in weight. 'Once you lose the fins, bones and guts, there is only about 325 g (11 oz) of cooked fish on each one.'

He holds one up to show the class. 'Watch the "get-away-from-you" fin. It's a fearsome spike that can lead to a bad infection if you are stabbed by it. Make sure you remove all the fins from the fish as they will burn on the char-grill like hair.' For this he uses a pair of scissors.

Damien also advises washing the fish and patting it dry before cooking. 'This removes any stray scales and, after all, you don't really know where it's been

The class laughs but he's making a serious point: 'Think about it: it may have been dropped on the floor at some point.'

Damien continues showing the engrossed audience (several of whom are rapidly developing a crush on the young chef) how to prepare the fish. 'The rule used to be that you only scored the sides of oily fish, not white ones, before barbecuing or grilling, but today I want you to score each side of these fish three or four times. This will ensure that they cook evenly.'

He instructs the class to oil the fish, not the grill plate. 'And don't use too much oil. You want just a little lubrication so that it doesn't stick, but doesn't create loads of black smoke either.'

OPPOSITE: THE SUSHI AND SASHIMI WORKSHOP IS ONE OF THE MOST POPULAR AND TAKES PLACE UNDER THE GUIDANCE OF A SUSHI MASTER CHEF.

RIGHT: EARLY MORNING TOURS OF THE MARKET ARE ALSO AVAILABLE.

Desensitized by years manning professional ovens, Damien adeptly turns the half-cooked fish using his bare hands and an egg flip. 'I do it this way because it's easier for me,' he says. 'A lot of people at home would use tongs and an egg flip. Remember: don't turn the fish too much during cooking. If you try and turn it too early, especially if the barbecue is not hot enough, it will stick. You want to get big black lines right along the fish. Use your knife to take a peek inside as they can take anything from five to 12 minutes to cook on each side depending on the shape of the individual fish.'

Demonstration completed, the owner of one of Australia's premier boutique wine companies steps forward to tell the class a little about the chardonnay she has chosen to accompany Damien's dish. Participants then move to the kitchen next door to try and replicate what they have just been shown. Damien and the staff at the Seafood School move from station to station answering questions, reminding people of the next step in the recipe and helping them find the equipment.

The class attracts all ranges of abilities yet everyone is a little nervous at first in the unfamiliar kitchen, working alongside strangers. By the time everyone sits down to eat the delicious results of their efforts, the mood is relaxed and jovial. There is plenty of that excellent chardonnay to be had, and still time to stop at a café on the way home for desserts and digestifs.

Courses currently available

Evening classes including:
*Australian Gourmet Traveller &
The Wine Magazine* — In this course, learn the key to successful wine matching and recipes. This team presents wine-friendly seafood recipes at this exciting hands-on dinner class.

Day courses including:
Seafood BBQ — The most popular class at the school where you can learn how to barbecue fish, shellfish and squid to perfection.

Two-day and Four-day courses including:
Strictly Seafood — A comprehensive course covering the fundamentals of preparation, storage, species identification and cooking methods. Great for anyone who wants to gain more confidence in handling fish and shellfish.

Contact: Sydney Seafood School
Sydney Fish Market
Bank Street
Pyrmont
Sydney NSW 2009
Tel +61 (0)2 9004 1140
Fax +44 (0)2 9004 1144
www.sydneyfishmarket.com.au

Wine Country Cooking
School, Ontario, Canada

Jane Langdon is a high-flyer in the public relations business in Toronto. Wine Country Cooking school is her hobby, yet it is far from amateur. Jane holds a degree in food and nutrition, and worked for a culinary academy during her final year of study. Somewhat disillusioned by the classicism of the teaching there, she never thought she would work at a cooking school again, until she saw that the things she did not like about it were in fact her opportunity: to provide entertaining yet educational classes for enthusiastic home cooks. And the spacious buildings at her husband Joe Will's new winery provided the perfect venue.

One of the oldest towns in Canada, Niagara-on-the-Lake is the former capital of the area previously known as Upper Canada. When the mist isn't too heavy, the U.S. (upstate New York in fact) can be seen stretching right along the opposite riverbank, stopping only when the body of water segues into the expanse of Lake Ontario.

A lot of the year it's pretty darn cold up there, but it is the proximity to this huge body of water that makes the comparatively small Niagara district ideal for certain types of wine production when other superficially similar regions are not. Lake Ontario is deep, so total sheet freeze is rare in winter, unlike nearby Lake Erie, where total sheet freeze is normal and the air circulation not as good. Just a few degrees of temperature make the difference.

Niagara-on-the-Lake is the heart of Canada's growing region for what they call 'tender fruit' — berries, peaches, plums, nectarines, apples, and grapes. The first wineries were established in

1860—1890, but most of the grape varieties chosen by these pioneering viticulturalists were not ideal. Wars and prohibition meant the industry failed to take off, until the mid-1970s when a new winery licence was granted to a team set on proving it was possible to make good wine in Ontario. Now there are more than 50 wineries on the peninsula, and within the next two years the number of wineries in Niagara-on-the-Lake is expected to reach 20.

Today the range of grape varieties is typically New World, but with a few key exceptions. It's a great area for Riesling and Gewurztraminer. Cabernet Franc grows so well here that it is made into a varietal wine rather than used simply in blends. And the negative — bloody cold weather — is here turned into a virtue with the production of award-winning white and red varieties of Icewine. Unlike Germany and Austria, Ontario is pretty much guaranteed each year to have weather cold enough to freeze the grapes naturally on the vine without being so cold that it kills the plant.

THE NATURAL WONDER OF NIAGARA FALLS IS A

15 MINUTE DRIVE FROM THE WINERY.

Cabernet Chicken with Celeriac Mash and Lemon Asparagus

SERVES 4

8 boneless, skinless chicken thighs

4 tablespoons blackberry jam

125 ml (4 fl oz) (½ cup) medium-bodied
Cabernet or Cabernet-blend wine

1 teaspoon grated lemon zest, plus the
    juice of 1 large lemon

1 teaspoon Dijon mustard

1 tablespoon olive oil

1 tablespoon finely chopped fresh ginger

1 tablespoon chopped fresh chives

1 garlic clove, finely chopped

fresh chives and blackberries, to garnish
    (optional)

FOR THE CELERIAC MASH

1 celeriac (celery root), about 500 g (1 lb)

3 Russet potatoes or other floury potatoes,
    about 500 g (1 lb)

1 tablespoon unsalted butter, cubed

60–125 ml (2–4 fl oz) (¼–½ cup) milk or
    vegetable stock

salt and pepper

FOR THE LEMON ASPARAGUS

1 bunch of asparagus, about 500 g (1 lb),
    trimmed

grated zest of ½ lemon

salt and freshly ground blalck pepper

This truly seasonal dish works in that difficult early spring period when so little is available. It fuses the last of winter's root vegetables with the first asparagus of the year. Jane recommends an asparagus steamer for best results. If you don't have one, cook it in a large shallow pan with 1.5 cm (¾ inch) water, covered, for 5 minutes.

To make the mash, have a large saucepan of fresh water ready. Peel the celeriac and cut it into 2.5 cm (1 inch) pieces, adding them to the pan of water as soon as possible, to prevent browning. Peel the potatoes and cut them into cubes slightly larger than the celeriac, then add them to the pan too.

Bring to a boil, then reduce the heat and allow to cook for about 20 minutes or until the vegetables are soft.

Meanwhile, prepare the chicken thighs, trimming the excess fat if desired. In a small bowl, combine the jam, wine, lemon zest, lemon juice and mustard. Stir to combine then set aside.

Heat the olive oil in a large wide frying pan or skillet over a medium heat. Add the ginger and chives and gently fry for about 2 minutes or until softened. Add the garlic and gently fry for 1 minute longer.

Push the flavouring ingredients to the edge of the pan and lay the chicken thighs in the pan, seam-side up. Cook for 3 minutes until golden on one side, then turn and cook for 3 minutes on the other side.

Meanwhile, drain the celeriac and potatoes thoroughly and return to the saucepan. Set aside in a warm place.

Pour the sauce mixture over the chicken. Cover and cook over a medium-low heat for 7 minutes. Uncover the pan, turn the chicken thighs over and continue cooking uncovered for 5 minutes so that the sauce can reduce and thicken. Spoon the sauce over the chicken from time to time to keep it moist.

Meanwhile, tie the trimmed asparagus bunch together with kitchen twine, using a quick-release knot. Place asparagus upright in the basket of an asparagus steamer. Add 2.5 cm (1 inch) water to the steamer pot and bring to a boil. Add the basket of asparagus. Cover and cook for 6–7 minutes.

Mash the celeriac and potatoes together. Add the butter and stir until melted, then add milk or vegetable stock until the desired consistency is achieved. Season to taste with salt and pepper and warm through as necessary.

Drain the asparagus when cooked. To serve, divide amongst warmed serving plates and sprinkle with the lemon zest, plus salt and pepper. Divide the mash and chicken between the plates. Spoon the sauce over the chicken, garnishing with fresh chives and blackberries if desired.

PARTICIPANTS WORK IN TEAMS OF TWO IN THE
SPACIOUS, WELL-EQUIPPED KITCHEN.

PARTICIPANTS WORK IN TEAMS OF TWO IN THE
SPACIOUS, WELL-EQUIPPED KITCHEN.

There is plenty here for wine enthusiasts to find interesting, and it was recognizing the unique assets Niagara-on-the-Lake producers had to offer tourists that fuelled Jane Langdon's interest in opening a cooking school on the premises of her husband's business, Strewn Winery, housed in a former fruit-canning factory.

Her aim is to provide '100 per cent recreational classes for people who want an entertaining and educational food and wine experience'. Recognizing the emerging importance of wine tourism, her ingredients and recipes tend to reflect the culinary background of this very special area. Classes are run every weekend from March until the end of November. Some are one-day affairs, starting at 10am and ending with a leisurely lunch. Others are designed as two-day programmes, with an early kick-off so that there is plenty of time for visiting local food producers or enjoying a tutored wine tasting in the afternoon.

Although the cooking school is Jane's hobby, her motto is 'if you are not going to do it properly, don't do it'. Consequently this is an exceptionally well-conceived and designed school. The ovens are semi-professional, the knives are by J.A. Henckels, the pots and pans are Analon Professional and Circulon, the roomy work stations are laden with quality gadgets, and there is space enough for everybody to cook dishes from scratch working in teams of two.

Clearing away and washing up are handled by two teaching assistants, a young human washer-upper and a highly desirable seven-minute industrial dishwashing machine.

On Jane's one-day 'Vintage Niagara' course, the themes are food and wine matching, and cooking with wine. 'The prime directive is: you have to drink what you like,' she reassures the group.

The menu she has chosen starts with lemon and dill crêpes, filled with a cream cheese mixture and leaves of Canadian smoked salmon. These are to be sliced diagonally and served as pre-dinner nibbles with the company's outstanding Riesling, though as winemaker Joe Will

LEFT: RED GRAPE VARIETIES TYPICAL OF THE AREA
INCLUDE CABERNET SAUVIGNON, CABERNET FRANC,
MERLOT AND PINOT NOIR.

OPPOSITE: THE CLOCK TOWER IN NIAGRA-ON-THE-LAKE.

reveals, the crêpes would also work well with Sauvignon Blanc or Pinot Grigio. 'There are two ways you could go with this,' he says. 'You are either looking for a wine that is compatible with a dish in terms of flavour and texture, or you want a palate-cleansing contrast.'

There follows a chargrilled Portobello mushroom salad. 'This is the most wine-friendly salad I know,' says Jane. 'Salad is hard to match with wine because the acidity in the salad dressing can make the wine taste flat and flabby. The dressing and marinade mixture we will be making today contains red wine rather than vinegar. We'll also be making a chicken dish with red wine to highlight the fact that you don't have to serve white wines with chicken.'

Jane emphasizes the importance of getting everything prepared before cooking begins. 'First do the stuff you have to concentrate on: the measuring, the chopping, the putting ingredients together,' she says. 'It makes life so much easier. You will also find that cooking is more relaxing and the results better because you are then just cooking.'

Throughout the class she reveals the tips and techniques that make the difference between okay and delicious. For successful chargrilling, we need to buy flat, broad Portobello mushrooms so that they cook evenly. 'Just put them on the heat and let them cook,' says Jane. 'They should spend 95 per cent of the cooking time with the gill-side down to avoid leatheriness. Think of it as benign neglect.

Make sure you get the marinade right into the gills so that they don't turn crispy on the grill.'

To finish the meal, and the day, our molten chocolate cakes are paired first with what Joe describes as 'a very un-Merlot-like Merlot' full of coffee and chocolate flavours, then an Icewine that marries equally well but differently. 'It's not a very sweet dessert, so you could argue you don't need a sweet wine. Or you could say it's a good mix with a sweet wine.' That's not a conclusion, but a great introduction to a fascinating sphere of gastronomy.

Other courses available

One-day classes
Timeless Classics – How to prepare a menu intended to evoke fond memories that stand the test of time.
Provencal Cuisine – In this class you learn to create a wonderful Provence-inspired three-course menu.

Vintage Culinary Weekend
Perfect for food and wine lovers involving hands-on cooking and lots of eating. Learn to cook a three-course lunch, matched with Strewn wines. Includes a wine appreciation session.

Culinary Vacation
The five-day (Mon-Fri) course includes daily cooking classes, producer and market visits, wine tastings, and dinner on Wednesday night at one of the region's top restaurants. Optional accommodation is available.

Contact: Wine Country Cooking School
1339 Lakeshore Road RR#3
Niagara-on-the-Lake
Ontario
Canada LoS 1Jo
Tel +1 905-468-8304
Fax +1 905-468-8305
www.winecountrycooking.com

Aldeburgh Cookery School,
Suffolk, England

Two hour's drive from London, Aldeburgh is a pretty old English seaside town with pastel-painted houses, cosy B&Bs, elegant shopping, good restaurants, great local beers, and long relaxing walks along the cobbled beach. Another key attraction: Aldeburgh Cookery School, run by food writer Thane Prince and local restaurateur Sara Fox, a friendly duo whose aim is to put enjoyment, conversation and passion back into cooking.

You may think you've signed up for a class in fish cookery, pasta, Moroccan or Thai cuisine, but the first thing you're going to do at Aldeburgh Cookery School is make bread with fresh yeast. It gives participants a chance to get to know each other and helps Thane and Sara illustrate a favourite point, that cooking is alchemy, and you can turn simple ingredients into gold.

The school occupies a charming stone cottage right on the high street with the ground floor specially converted to suit the ladies' style of teaching. On the right is a spacious kitchen, not unlike a large home kitchen, where guests work communally. The left side features a teaching and preparation area. Upstairs is the dining room and a small seating area for morning coffee and introductions. Something of a celebrity thanks to years of writing for the top-selling *Daily Telegraph* newspaper, plus appearances on television programmes and at the cookery demonstration theatres of various popular exhibitions such as the BBC Good Food Show, Thane bounds into the sitting room to outline the day's session and a few sensible guidelines about working safely in a busy kitchen. It's not intimidating: remember the knives are very sharp, call a warning when you are moving a hot pan of water across a room, and try to keep things tidy as you work.

THE BEACH AT ALDEBURGH, SUFFOLK, ENGLAND.

Mackerel with Orange and Pine Nut Stuffing

Thane and Sara have taken their inspiration from Sicily for this sophisticated mackerel dish with zesty stuffing. 'Being an oily fish, mackerel is best eaten as soon as possible after it is caught,' says Thane. 'The browning of the stuffing ingredients gives a sweet taste and crisp texture to the dish.'

SERVES 4

4 medium mackerel, gutted

6 tablespoons olive oil

2 tablespoons chopped shallot

100 g (3½ oz) (2 cups) white breadcrumbs

55 g (2 oz) (⅓ cup) pine nuts

2 garlic cloves, chopped

a handful of chopped fresh parsley

grated zest of 2 oranges

juice of 1 orange

sea salt and freshly ground black pepper

½ teaspoon caster sugar (optional)

Preheat the oven to 180°C (350°F) Gas Mark 4. Using a sharp knife, fillet the mackerel. Cut away any bones from the sides and middle of the fish, feeling the flesh with your fingertips to check where the bones are, then remove them.

Heat 3 tablespoons of olive oil in a frying pan, add the shallots and fry, stirring occasionally, over a medium-low heat until golden. Add the breadcrumbs, pine kernels and garlic and continue cooking and stirring until they too have some colour.

Add the parsley and orange zest and gently fry for a few more minutes. Remove the pan from the heat, add the orange juice, then taste and season as required with salt and freshly ground black pepper. If the orange juice is tart, add a little caster sugar.

Place one fillet from each fish skin-side down in a baking dish. Use a spoon to divide the stuffing amongst the fillets, pressing it down gently. Then put the remaining mackerel fillets 'head to tail' (each facing opposite each other) on top.

Drizzle the remaining 3 tablespoons of olive oil over the fish and bake in the preheated oven for 20 minutes or until cooked through. Serve hot or at room temperature with a crisp salad or freshly cooked green vegetables.

RIGHT: FILLETING DEMANDS NIMBLE FINGERS.

FAR RIGHT: THANE GARNISHES THE BREAD.

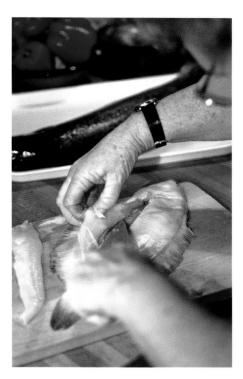

Since opening the school in 1999, Thane and Sara have built an enviable network of local food suppliers. Vegetables are grown to their specification, and fish is purchased direct from the boats lining the beach, so students have the opportunity to prepare and eat the best available. The wind may be chilly and clouds threatening, but the eight-strong class is excited to gather around the fisherman's hut as Dean talks to Thane and Sara about the morning's catch. He holds up a huge cod for inspection. 'Look at the eyes on that, bright and shining,' says Thane to the group. 'We'll have the bones as well Dean, when you wrap him up,' says Sara, who will be demonstrating how to make fish stock a little later.

The ladies want their guests to leave knowing how to recognize the best fish and how to prepare it. Thane holds up a large salmon and waggles its tail. 'You can tell very easily that this is a farmed fish because it's got a floppy, flabby tail and fins. Now look at the mackerel.' She holds the smaller, firmer fish up so everyone can see. 'It's got E-type, go-faster fins because it has been swimming freely. The salmon's flesh is not as firm and muscular.'

The kitchen assistants lay the array of fish on trays in the teaching room. Standing around a large work table, we begin filleting the fish step-by-step to Sara's steady instruction, while Thane offers tips,

jokes and anecdotes. She's very serious about wanting people to develop their knife skills however. 'The prep work can be as enjoyable as the toss-it-in-the-pan stuff if you know how to do it professionally,' she says. Thane also emphasizes that the way an ingredient is cut can actually alter the taste of the dish, not just the appearance and texture, and spends a significant part of the day showing how best to use knives to chop a variety of vegetables and herbs.

A typical 'Great British Fish' class would include dishes such as goujons of sole. fillets of Dover sole with tarragon cream sauce, home-salted cod with wilted greens, skate with black butter, and baked

ABOVE: FRESH FISH IS ALWAYS AVAILABLE FROM THE LOCAL BEACH.

RIGHT: A FISHERMAN AT WORK.

mackerel with orange and pine nut stuffing. 'The subject forms the core of the day but you cook everything you eat, including the biscuits you will have with coffee,' says Thane. There's no testing or being put on the spot — the emphasis is firmly on relaxation and enjoyment as well as inspiration and education.

The days finish with a leisurely, boozy banquet of dishes prepared during the session and lots of gossip about restaurants. Thane can't resist talking about her experiences working with some of Britain's most prestigious chefs and happily takes the mickey out of herself as much as them. Her no-nonsense manner is tempered by a risqué sense of humour so no one is surprised to learn that she was a hospital ward sister before becoming a professional foodie.

The kindly Sara is a little more reserved yet Thane makes it clear that one of the great attractions of opening the school in Aldeburgh was the opportunity to work with this extremely knowledgeable and experienced chef.

FRESHLY CAUGHT SCALLOPS MAKE A DELICIOUS DINNER.

Masterclasses lead by Thane go more deeply into a specific subject such as bread or pasta and include a great deal of sampling, with a balanced lunch supplied in addition to the food cooked in class. Weekend courses include five hands-on cooking sessions plus lunch at Sara's cosy restaurant, The Lighthouse. 'The weekends give you the chance to spend time with people who will talk endlessly about food, and to ask as many questions as you want,' says Thane. In fact, that's a fair description of any course at this friendly and unpretentious school.

Also in the U.K.
Caroline Yates of Confident Cooking offers friendly communal cooking sessions in Wiltshire with relaxing residential weekend courses available. See www.confidentcooking.com. In the far southwest of England, Rick Stein's cookery school offers a special focus on fish in a spectacular setting. Visit www.rickstein.com for details. To get a grip on modern Aga cookery, try Amy Willcock's sessions on the Isle of Wight. See www.amywillcock.co.uk for details.

Courses currently available

One-day courses including:
Italian — A hands-on class sampling dishes such as risotto nero and tiramisu as well as tasting Italian oils and making fresh pasta.

Weekend courses including:
Modern British Food — Three days of cooking, eating, drinking and discussing food and wine, including visits to local producers, sampling beer from local breweries and five cooking sessions. No accommodation included.

Contact: Aldeburgh Cookery School
84 High Street
Aldeburgh
Suffolk
IP15 5AB
Tel: +44 (0)1728 454039
www.aldeburghcookeryschool.com

Betty's Cookery School, Harrogate, England

The British tradition of afternoon tea is much-admired around the world but has sadly fallen from favour in its country of origin. Yes, grand hotels offer it daily, but at an alarming cost, even when considering that London is the second most expensive city in the world. (In fact, if you want to enjoy a truly fine hotel tea you are better off visiting the colonial-style hotels of Asia.) Cream teas can still be found on offer throughout much of Devon and Cornwall, but as with London hotels, custom is primarily tourists and other holidaymakers, and the quality can be disappointing. You don't sense that here is something the British enjoy regularly, and sometimes you don't blame them.

Visit Yorkshire however and you will see local people happily queuing, even in the rain, for afternoon tea at Betty's. This small group of elegant yet friendly tearooms was founded in 1919 by Frederick Belmont, a Swiss confectioner who came to England to seek his fortune.

Although he adopted local specialities with enthusiasm, Frederick and his descendants have retained many traditions of continental European patisserie and confectionery. The result is a menu in which Fat Rascals (a comforting mound of sweet dough studded with citrus peel, vine fruits, cherries and almonds) and Yorkshire Parkin (a moist dark loaf cake made

with black treacle, oatmeal and ginger), sit alongside frangipane fruit tarts and a modernized rendition of the Austrian favourite Linzertorte.

Betty's principle of making everything from scratch means that, over the years, the company has built up an impressive team of specialists. These include chefs, master bakers, confectioners, and tea and coffee experts, many of whom have trained and worked in Switzerland as well as in other countries. In 2001 Betty's opened a cookery school in Harrogate, on the site of its craft bakery, with the dual aim of training its own staff and using the expertise of its top people to teach enthusiastic customers.

A TRADITIONAL ENGLISH AFTERNOON TEA AT BETTY'S.

Any concerns you may have about the school being situated on an industrial estate on the outskirts of town are dispelled as soon as you enter the building. Betty's pristine premises are spacious, stylish and luxurious. The front demonstration point has up-to-the-minute video facilities allowing detailed close-ups of the food preparation and in-pan action.

Most important however is the fact that every student has his or her own generously proportioned workstation (with enviable black granite worktop and roomy stainless steel oven), so during practical classes, each student makes every dish. This is rare amongst cooking schools and maximises the opportunity to learn, practise and acquire skills during your visit. A typical one-day practical class runs from 9 am–4 pm.

For the demonstration-only sessions, which last about three hours, the maximum number of students increases from 18 to 24.

Though manager and head teacher Victoria Crebbin is quietly pleased at the success of all classes, she stresses that the most popular ones are based on foods for which Betty's is renowned: baking in its myriad forms, chocolate and traditional Swiss dishes. Those attending the chocolate class learn the fundamental skills of tempering and moulding chocolate, how to make ganache plus a variety of chocolate desserts. The Swiss Specialities class includes rösti, Swiss chocolate torte (see recipe opposite) and Rüebli torte (a moist carrot cake made with ground almonds). The company's tea experts offer occasional masterclasses in which participants learn about the

Swiss Chocolate Torte

This very rich cake should be served in small slices and, for best results, made two days in advance. Ground almonds can be used instead of hazelnuts if desired. To make a larger cake, double the recipe, use a 30 cm (12 inch) cake ring, and bake for 40 minutes.

SERVES 6–12

melted butter, for greasing

plain (all-purpose) flour, for dusting

75 g (3 oz) dark (semisweet) chocolate

1 tablespoon cold water

60 g (2 oz) (¼ cup) butter

3 eggs, separated

90 g (3½ oz) (scant 1 cup) ground hazelnuts

1½ teaspoon kirsch

a pinch of salt

30 g (3 tablespoons) caster (superfine) sugar

FOR THE TOPPING

75 g (3 oz) dark, semi-sweet chocolate

60 ml (2 fl oz) (¼ cup) soured cream or crème fraîche

cocoa powder, for dusting (optional)

Heat the oven to 180°C (350°F) Gas 4. Lay a sheet of non-stick baking parchment on a baking sheet. Butter and flour the inside of a 16 cm (6½ inch) cake ring, then sit it on the baking parchment.

Break up the chocolate and place in a heavy-bottomed saucepan. Add the water and allow the chocolate to melt over a very gentle heat, stirring until smooth.

Remove the pan from the heat and whisk in the butter and egg yolks. Stir in the ground nuts and the kirsch, then set the chocolate mixture aside.

In a large bowl, whisk the egg whites and salt together until stiff peaks form. Add the sugar and continue beating until the mixture is meringue-like. Gently fold the chocolate mixture into the egg whites.

Pour the batter into the prepared cake ring and bake for about 25 minutes or until risen and firm. Remove from the oven and set aside to cool.

To make the topping, place a heatproof bowl over a small pan of hot water on the stovetop. Add the chocolate to the bowl and allow it to melt. Mix in the soured cream or crème fraîche.

When the cake has cooled, lift the ring off and remove the paper from the base. Use a palette knife or metal spatula to spread the topping over the cake. If you wish, dust lightly with cocoa powder.

LEFT: BETTY'S RECOMMEND USING A SMALL PAPER CONE FOR INTRICATE WORK SUCH AS PIPING BITE-SIZED CHOCOLATES AS IT HELPS THE COOK MAINTAIN CONTROL.

OPPOSITE LEFT: ALL STUDENTS HAVE THEIR OWN SPACIOUS WORKSTATION.

OPPOSITE RIGHT: AN ALL-DAY PRACTICAL CLASS INCLUDES THREE BREAKS FOR REFRESHMENTS.

different varieties of tea, how to taste for quality, distinguish between the various flavours, and actually blend their own tea as part of the session. Betty's is also acquiring a reputation for its children's holiday classes, which aim to provide young people with the enthusiasm to cook as well as teach them basic kitchen skills in a safe and happy environment.

Victoria heads up the Tea Time Treats practical class herself, and aims to show how the quaint tradition of afternoon tea can move with the times. There are scones, of course, but they are flavoured with Parmesan and chives. The loaf cake is an intriguing combination of courgettes (zucchinis), pistachios and walnuts. An orange-flavoured almond cake is

brimming with sweet wine and vodka. Throughout the day there are breaks for tea and coffee and more Betty's goodies. When it's all over, students leave laden with boxes and bags filled with the items made by their own fair hands. Victoria and her colleagues carefully choose the recipes so that not everything that's taken home has to be consumed in one day — though obviously some folk try.

'People today perhaps don't take afternoon tea as much as they could or should,' says Victoria. So what's Yorkshire got that keeps this tradition so vibrantly alive? 'There is a slower pace of life here, and we are so renowned for making cakes, we've got to find the time to eat them all as well.'

If you are interested in this course you may also want to try the Bread Matters classes at Melmerby in the Lake District, run by organic pioneer and artisan baker Andrew Whitley. In addition to classes in the fundamentals of baking, Whitley offers specialised courses such as Russian Baking, The Perfect Sourdough and Baking for a Gluten-free Diet. See www.breadmatters.com. A short drive from Betty's Cookery School is the hotel Swinton Park, based in a spectacular castle. There respected chef and teacher Rosemary Shrager conducts hands-on one-day and residential classes in a variety of subjects including Modern British, Game, Summer Food and Back to Basics with special deals for non-cooking partners. See www.swintonpark.co.uk

Courses currently available

One-day courses including:
Swiss Specialities – Betty's most popular course covers how to make the perfect rösti and other savoury and sweet dishes.
Perfect Puddings – How to make hot, cold, simple and sophisticated puddings for every occasion.
One Pot Wonders – A variety of warming and comforting dishes including traditional English favourites for easy kitchen supper entertaining.

Ten-day courses including:
Betty's Certificate Course – A practical course covering knife skills, starters, main courses, desserts, vegetables, breadmaking and cakes, and table service. Tutorials are provided on menu planning, time management, catering for large numbers and culinary tips. All meals included. No accommodation included.

Contact: Betty's Cookery School
Hookstone Park
Hookstone Chase
Harrogate
North Yorkshire HG2 7LD
Tel +44 (0)1423 814016
Fax +44 (0)1423 814017
www.bettyscookeryschool.co.uk

Walnut Grove Cookery School, Loire, France

The myriad waterways running through the Loire Valley region are not just a scenic delight, they produce fertile soil that has made this one of the most important centres of fruit and vegetable growing in France. Add the magnificent châteaux of the 15th and 16th centuries, fine wines and wine vinegars, fresh and dried mushrooms, an appreciation of organic food production and a tradition of farmhouse cheese making, and it is easy to see why Maynard and Freya Harvey were tempted to move here and set up a cookery school.

Chicken liver parfait with sweet and sour sauce and warm brioche, salmon with poached egg, crushed new potatoes, asparagus tips and hollandaise, caramelized pear crème brûlée with pistachio shortbread, plus sorbet, cheese and petits fours. It sounds like a menu from an elegant Michelin-starred restaurant, but the chef who'll be cooking it is, well, you. That is, if you book for a five-day cookery course at Walnut Grove Cookery School.

Set in the Mayenne area close to the border with Brittany, an hour and a half drive from the port of St Malo, or a two-hour train trip from Paris, Walnut Grove Cookery School was established in 2003 and takes its name from the trees surrounding the idyllic rural property. The school is owned by Maynard and Freya Harvey, who work with business partner and long-time friend and colleague Benedict Haines. After selling their elegant gastro-pub Seland Newydd near Brecon in Wales, Maynard and Freya, who met on a holiday tour in Colombia, decided to move their young family to France. They spent some time focusing on renovating their new home, then in 2001 purchased the farmhouse property that is now the cookery school and ran it as a gîte until they were ready to launch their teaching programme. It is still possible to hire Walnut Grove for luxury gourmet breaks rather than cooking courses.

Classes are taught by Maynard and Benedict, who between them have many years of experience in the restaurant business, in the kitchen and front of house. They met when both worked at a hotel in Wales 12 years ago. Freya handles much of the administration of the school, and takes guests to visit local food producers and places of interest. Guests stay in ensuite bedrooms with exposed beams and open log fires. The spacious, professionally equipped kitchen is set across the courtyard from the farmhouse and has been purpose-designed for the use of the students.

The cuisine favoured by Maynard and Benedict is contemporary, emphasizing fresh ingredients, distinct flavours and meticulous elegant presentation. With a

THE FRESH FRUIT IN THE LOCAL MARKET.

Passion Fruit and Orange Bavarois with a Caramel Cage

SERVES 4

FOR THE BAVAROIS

100 ml (3½ fl oz) (scant ½ cup) milk

200 ml (scant 1 cup) double (heavy) cream

6 tablespoons caster (superfine) sugar

3 egg yolks

2 leaves gelatine, cut up and soaked in
   cold water

200 ml (scant 1 cup) orange juice

4 passion fruit, plus 2 extra to decorate

FOR THE CARAMEL CAGES

400 g (13 oz) (2 cups) granulated white sugar

225 ml (7½ fl oz) (1 cup) water

225 ml (7½ fl oz) (1 cup) liquid glucose

The artful presentation of desserts such as this is a key skill that guests learn at Walnut Grove. Make sure you use ripe passion fruit for this deliciously creamy yet tangy dessert. The quantities given here for the caramel cages will make more than you need to serve on one occasion, but it is not really worth working with a smaller amount. Store the excess cages carefully in an airtight box lined with paper towels.

To prepare the bavarois, combine the milk, half of the cream and 1 tablespoon of the caster sugar in a medium saucepan. Place over a medium-high heat and bring to scalding point.

Meanwhile, whisk together the egg yolks and remaining sugar, until pale and fluffy.

Just before the milk mixture comes to the boil, pour a little of it over the yolks, whisking it constantly. Then pour all the yolk mixture into the saucepan and heat slowly, stirring continuously with a wooden spoon until the custard thickens enough to leave a thick line on the back of the spoon when you run your finger across it.

Remove the pan from the heat. Squeeze the excess water from the softened gelatine and add it to the custard, whisking

thoroughly. Pour the custard through a chinois or very fine sieve, into a mixing bowl, then set aside to cool, stirring often.

Combine the orange juice and passion fruit pulp in a clean saucepan and bring to a boil over a high heat. Boil the mixture hard to reduce and thicken it. When you have a syrupy mixture of 150 ml (¼ pint) (⅔ cup) volume, remove the pan from the heat and leave it to cool.

In another mixing bowl, half-whip the remaining cream and put to one side. Fold the passion-fruit mixture into the custard, then fold in the semi-whipped cream. Pour the mixture into four moulds each 175 ml (6 fl oz) or smaller if desired, and leave to set in refrigerator.

To make the caramel cages, combine the sugar and water in a small, heavy-based saucepan. Bring to the boil then

add the glucose and cook until the mixture becomes a light amber colour.

Meanwhile, prepare a basin of iced water. Remove the caramel from the heat and dip only the bottom of the pan into the iced water for 5 to 10 seconds. Set aside to cool at room temperature.

The caramel should now be thick and honey-like. If necessary, place on a low heat to maintain the proper consistency.

Dip a teaspoon into the caramel and drizzle it back and forth over the back of a stainless-steel ladle to create a cage shape. When set hard, gently lift off the cage and set aside while you repeat with the remaining caramel.

Turn out each mould onto serving plates. Cut the extra passion fruits in half, and set one half on top of each bavarois. Cover with the caramel cages and serve.

ratio of four students to one chef, and a maximum of eight guests in attendance, the degree of personal attention is high, so although you might not believe it, you really can get to grips with confits, bavarois and terrines by the end of the week.

A typical programme: on the day of arrival guests are given an introductory talk, then treated to champagne and a six-course gourmet dinner. Next morning after breakfast it's straight into a hands-on lesson in breads, brioche and croissants. Guests normally work together in groups of two or three. There follows a demonstration class on purchasing and preparing fish, then it's back to the hands-on cooking again as students begin

preparation of the evening's menu. That's all before the lunch break. In the afternoon there is a visit to an artisan cheese producer, then a demonstration on working with chocolate, and the final hands-on session of the day, which focuses on the finishing and presentation of the evening meal.

A similar pattern is followed for the next three days, featuring visits to producers, demonstrations in preparation of meat, stocks, pasta, ice creams and preserves, and daily hands-on sessions that culminate in six-course restaurant-style dinners. The practical session on the final day is structured so that guests use all the skills and knowledge they have

acquired during the week to cook and present dinner as a group with minimal input from the chefs. It's not so much a test as a team challenge, the pressure relieved somewhat by a barbecue lunch and a relaxing afternoon of games such as croquet and boules.

Maynard and Benedict believe that everyone is capable of skilfully combining flavours and textures, and presenting dishes well. 'Enjoying cooking is all about confidence, being relaxed and understanding your ingredients,' says Maynard. 'Our aim at the Walnut Grove is to bring these qualities out, so that you have the ability to follow your own flair and imagination.'

ABOVE: A TRIO OF SWEETS, INCLUDING PASSIONFRUIT AND ORANGE BAVAROIS.

ABOVE AND RIGHT: FRESH LOCAL PRODUCE AS SEEN DURING VISITS TO THE LOCAL MARKETS.

Freya meanwhile is mindful that guests are visiting Walnut Grove on holiday. Originally from New Zealand, she has a healthy list of proposed activities including visits to art galleries and the beautiful medieval town of Vitré, but realises that different things appeal to different people. One of the more unusual opportunities is a trip to a 19th-century windmill that processes buckwheat, called *sarrasin* or *blé noir* in French, the triangular grain that is best known for its use in galettes. There is also a trip to a small farm near the school where round, soft, fresh country-style cheeses are made from cows' milk, then left plain or coated in herbs or pepper. Guests watch these being made, as well as the traditional production of crème fraîche,

France's esteemed cultured soured cream, and learn how the remaining parts of the fresh milk are put to use.

The school hopes soon to offer a programme that focuses exclusively on wines and foods of the Loire region, which has been described as the least polluted area of France. It remains beautifully lush and features a great deal of wildlife. The historic grand châteaux of the area produce world-famous wines such as Anjou, Saumur, Muscadet, Sancerre, Vouvray and Pouilly Blanc Fumé. It is also famous for the production of goats' milk cheeses, particularly Sainte-Maure, Crottin de Chavignol and Selles-sur-Cher, which is distinctively covered with powdered charcoal.

There are several special varieties of pear associated with different parts of the Loire — the Comice was developed in Angers. Reinettes or Little Queens are an esteemed French apple, of which the Loire has traditional local strains including Reinette d'Orléans and Reine de Reinette. Reine-claude is the French word for greengage, which are also linked to the Loire area, as Queen Claude (wife of François I) was born in the Sologne district. Other regions of the country may be more commonly associated with gastronomy, but the Loire offers much for food lovers to explore and enjoy, and Walnut Grove is an ideal base.

Also in France

Anne Willan's La Varenne cooking school is based at the Château du Feÿ in Burgundy and is ideal for the serious cook who wants to learn as much as possible during their stay. For more information visit www.lavarenne.com. Learn how to cook with foie gras, magrets and confit at the week-long courses run in Marciac, Gascony, by Tasting Places. Accommodation is in an 18th century château. See www.tastingplaces.com for details.

VINEYARDS COVER THE LOIRE VALLEY JUST OUTSIDE THE TOWN OF SANCERRE.

This five-day cookery course is currently the only course on offer by Walnut Grove Cookery School.

Includes demonstrations, hands-on cooking and visits to local producers and tours of the local château and grounds. Accommodation included.

Contact: Walnut Grove Cookery School
Le Hunaudiere
53400
Livre la Touche
Mayenne
Tel: +33 (0) 2 43 98 50 02
www.walnutgrovecookery.com

Food Lover's Tour of Paris, Paris, France

Here is an opportunity to experience Paris through the eyes and palate of a discerning Frenchwoman. Paule Caillat first worked in the fashion industry as a buyer for Bergdorf Goodman in New York, but after several years dealing with some of the most prestigious brands in the fashion world, she decided to turn her beloved hobby, food, into her full-time profession. Now she guides small groups of visitors around the market of the Marais district, then takes them back to her elegant apartment to teach them to cook the fresh produce purchased. After a relaxing lunch with wine and cheese, she accompanies guests to leading stores in other parts of the city.

'Look at those strawberries, I would never buy them!' says Paule Caillat. The bright red, tall, pyramid-shaped fruit look spectacular on the market stall, but clearly don't meet with her approval. 'See: they're 1.20 euros a kilo. When I buy strawberries, even in season, they're 6 euros a kilo. These are too big, pumped full of water, full of chemicals. The strawberry season is May to July — even in August they're a little touchy.'

We certainly won't be buying them today, on a blustery Friday in February. Paule is very clear about the type of ingredients her group of four food-loving clients need to be guided to at the morning market near Oberkampf station: fresh, seasonal produce that is locally grown. Her one concession is juicy Moroccan lemons. 'In fact it is easy to see where the food comes from because, by law, it has to be shown on the product,' she counsels.

At another stall Paule points to dark, elongated beetroot (beets), the shape of thin aubergines (eggplants), and a nearby box of plump, creamy mushrooms. 'These are cultivated but they are very good.

We'll use them in the soufflé as well as the salad.' As she purchases them, we admire the picture-perfect bunches of thyme, flat-leaf parsley, mint, chervil, tarragon, chives and dill on display. These, and the bouquets of vivid green salad leaves, are extraordinarily clean.

'We are going to turn here,' Paule suddenly announces. 'I'm not buying cheese from that stall over there anymore. It's not that it's bad, it's just that the other place is better.' She nips behind us so that the jolly group conceals her as it strolls onwards. 'The problem is the stall holders know it's me whenever they see a group of more than two people walking around.'

At the favoured cheese stall, Paule has a brief chat with the owner. 'You can't be a specialist in everything,' she reassures us. 'My speciality is finding good things, but I'm going to discuss with her what goat cheese is best today, and I will buy a cows' milk cheese to contrast with it.'

We walk past a long queue of people waiting patiently for fish. 'France is secular but some of the old Catholic

ABOVE: SALAD IS SERVED ON CLASSIC
LEAF-SHAPED PLATES.

ABOVE RIGHT: PAULE DEMONSTRATES HER
FAMILY'S DISTINCTIVE PASTRY CRUST RECIPE.

traditions remain and one is that on Fridays people eat fish. However, fish has become very expensive, and this stall is busy because it is a discount fish stall.' It's not what foreigners tend to expect of the discerning Parisians, and certainly not what we are looking for today.

'Now this farmer is based near Paris and they just come in with what they have,' says Paule at a table full of different types of cabbage, celeriac and mâché. 'These French beans are much better than the ones we saw earlier. Look: they're smaller and more tender. The ends just snap off.'

Our tour of the stalls finished, Paule leads the group back to her chic apartment, via her favourite boulangerie. 'You're lucky,'

she says. "Last week it was closed, but it just happens to have the best baguette in the neighbourhood.' Still she discourages us from buying any pastries at the store. 'Boulangerie and pâtisserie are opposite trades that work in opposite atmospheres, one hot, one cold, so don't buy both at one shop. Pastries in a boulangerie may look good but they won't be the best.'

The spacious kitchen has granite work surfaces, limestone flooring, two sinks, two ovens, and a central table around which we sit in rattan armchairs for food preparation and dining. 'I have a motto,' says Paule, introducing the cooking session. 'No unnecessary steps, but all the necessary steps.' She passes around cutting boards and a collection of Global

Fruit Tart with Almond Cream

The Caillat Family Crust taught by Paule is an unusual but very easy means of making a rich pastry tart case. 'You just work it like Play-Doh and press it into the tart pan, making the crust as thick as you like.' she says. Paule favours Echiré butter from the Charentais for this recipe. 'It is fantastic for pastry. It has a high fat content and goes through a high-quality churning process, although is not essential for success.' The butter mixture could be brought to the boil in a microwave, but as the conventional oven needs to be heated in order to bake the tart, it is just as easy to do it there. To make a savoury pastry crust, simply omit the sugar. The ingredients here will fill a 22 cm (8½ inch) tart pan. Use a metal pan, rather than ceramic, to help the pastry crisp.

SERVES 6

FOR THE PASTRY

   80 g (3 oz) (¾ stick) unsalted butter

   3 tablespoons water

   1 tablespoon sunflower oil

   1 tablespoon sugar

   a pinch of salt

   plenty of pastry flour

FOR THE FILLING

   100 g (3½ oz) (½ cup) caster sugar

   100 g (3½ oz) (1 cup) ground almonds

   100 g (3½ oz) 1 stick unsalted butter, softened

   1 egg

   1 tablespoon plain (all-purpose) flour

   1 tablespoon rum or kirsch

   about 500 g (1 lb) summer fruit such as
      berries, redcurrants, apricots and peaches

   1 tablespoon icing (confectioners') sugar

To make the pastry, preheat the oven to 200°C (400°F) Gas Mark 6. In a Pyrex or other heatproof bowl, combine the butter, water, oil, sugar and salt, and place in the oven for about 15 minutes or until the mixture reaches boiling point.

Remove the bowl from the oven and add a few large spoonfuls of flour, stirring quickly to blend. Keep adding more spoonfuls of flour gradually, until the mixture forms a ball. Keep adding flour a spoonful at a time until the pastry no longer sticks to the side of the bowl.

Use your hands to spread the pastry out evenly to line the tart pan. Prick the base all over with a fork, then use the tines of the fork to neaten the sides of the pastry case by pressing it gently and evenly against the edge of the pan.

Bake the tart case for 10–15 minutes or until it is light brown and contains fine cracks. Remove from the oven and set aside ready to fill. Lower the oven temperature to 180°C (350°F) Gas Mark 4.

To make the filling, combine the sugar and ground almonds in a mixing bowl. Beat in the softened butter, then the egg, flour and rum or kirsch. Spoon the mixture into the baked pastry case. Bake for 20 minutes, then remove from the oven and set aside to cool.

Meanwhile, prepare the fruit, cutting it into attractive pieces if large, or simply trimming and leaving whole if small. Arrange the fruit as you wish over the tart and dust with icing sugar just before serving.

A PARISIAN ART MARKET.

knives so we can help slicing and dicing. The exquisite cheese and bread are put out for anyone who is already hungry.

Paule has taken into account each participant's likes and dislikes, and special culinary interests when planning the day's menu, which is a good mix of modern and traditional French styles. The starter is a mushroom soufflé, made special with the addition of fashionable tonka bean spice, grated into the mixture as commonly done with whole nutmeg.

'These rosé champignons are wonderful to eat raw too,' says Paule, 'but they are very sandy because they are cultivated in sand. You must discard the sandy stem, don't keep it and use it. These are the only mushrooms you should wash. I put lemon or vinegar in the water because the acidity helps to draw out the sand.'

The main course, chicken tagine, is a Moroccan dish but Paule is unrepentant. 'It's France's second cuisine. We feel very close to North African countries, and have been going to Morocco forever. It's nice and exotic, without being too exotic.'

She makes it in a traditional French cast-iron pot known as a *doufeu*. Unusually, the lid features a cavity. Ice cubes are placed in it to encourage condensation on the underside, which features several dimples to encourage the water to drip

back into the base of the pot. 'The drips are less necessary when you are doing a stew but make an amazing difference to pot-roast veal,' Paule explains.

For the optional after-lunch session, Paule takes students to a selection of the most esteemed food, wine and equipment stores in Paris, and is greeted warmly at each one. First is the evocative spice shop of Jean-Marie Thiercelin, where Troisgros, Robuchon and other leading French chefs come for saffron, tonka beans, fine vinegars and gourmet grains. Then to Stohrer, the oldest pâtisserie in Paris, and the famous wine shop and confectioner Legrand Filles et Fils, which has been operating for 120 years.

The day concludes with a journey into the basement of the Poilâne bakery in St-Germain-des-Prés to watch sourdough loaves being shunted into the ancient oven. For most of Paule's clients it is the highlight of their visit to Paris, and she speaks long and passionately about her admiration for the recently deceased Lionel Poilâne. Paule's Food Lover's Tour of Paris may be booked through Gourmet on Tour (see right for contact details).

Four times a year, American food writer Patricia Wells offers week-long courses in Paris. Visit www.patriciawells.com. Or go-it-alone with a personalized itinerary devised by *Time Out Paris* contributor Rosa Jackson. See www.edible-paris.com.

Courses currently available

One to five day courses including:
Ecole Ritz Escoffier – The Ritz Escoffier School is the highest realm of French gastronomy, with unparalleled excellence in instruction. This course can be tailormade between one and five days, or one week. No accommodation included.

At Home with Patricia Wells – Based in St Germain-des-Prés, award-winning food critic and author Patricia Wells invites guests into her kitchen studio for this five day course. The perfect week for those who want to appreciate the gastronomic bounty of Paris. No accommodation included.

Contact: Gourmet on Tour
Berkeley Square House
2F Berkeley Square
Mayfair
London W1J 6BD
Tel UK +44 (0)20 7396 5550
Fax UK +44 (0)20 7900 1527
Tel US 1 800 504 9842
Fax US 1 800 886 2229
www.gourmetontour.com

Château de Berne, Provence, France

Set in the Haute Var, a resolutely rural and resolutely French area just over an hour's drive from Nice and Marseilles airports, Château de Berne is actually owned by an Englishman, Bill Muddyman. Since buying the centuries-old wine estate 15 years ago, he has restored its vineyards, converted a house into a 19-room auberge, and in 2003 converted a separate building into a cookery school where guests learn about Provençal cooking from the auberge's chef, Jean-Louis Vosgien. Formerly of the Château de la Messardière in Saint Tropez, Jean-Louis' culinary style is a mix of cuisine du terroir (food 'of the soil') and cuisine grand-mère (grandmother's cooking). He uses organic vegetables, wild herbs and olive oil, grown in the château's gardens and olive grove, to encapsulate Provence on a plate. The estate also boasts L'Ecole du Vin, which offers guided tours of the vineyard followed by tutored wine tastings with the château's experts.

Let's give it the full name: L'Ecole de Cuisine du Château de Berne. It sounds very grand and formal but the aim of this school is to teach Provençal cooking in a relaxed and informal manner. Hidden away in the vineyards of a private 650-hectare wine estate, this idyllic venue is based in a little country house specially converted for cookery courses given in small groups. Olive trees, rosemary bushes and thyme plants are right on the doorstep. There is a shady terrace where guests can enjoy the food they have

prepared together in class, accompanied by wine from the estate, and luxury accommodation is right next door, in the Château de Berne's air-conditioned auberge.

Chef and teacher Jean-Louis Vosgien, who speaks English, says: 'First and foremost I don't exactly feel like "a teacher". Of course I do want to teach people how to prepare food and cook it, but when I am cooking during the classes I am not so much teaching, as sharing my knowledge. I cook more with my heart than with my

OPPOSITE: FIELDS OF LAVENDER, SUCH AS THESE IN VALENSOLE, ARE A COMMON SIGHT IN PROVENCE.

RIGHT: THE BALCONY VIEW OF THE L'AUBERGE HOTEL AND RESTAURANT.

Pissaladière

At Château de Berne, pissaladière, the classic Provençal flan, is made with puff pastry, although you can make it with bread dough if you prefer. Eat this hot straight from the oven, or let it cool to warm or room temperature. Serve in small pieces with aperitifs, or cut larger to serve as a main dish with a green salad.

SERVES 6–8

1.5 kg (3 lbs) white onions
a little olive oil
a few sprigs of thyme
salt and freshly ground black pepper
300 g (10 oz) puff pastry
10 anchovy fillets
15 black olives

Cut the onions into thin slices. Heat a large frying pan or skillet and pour a thin film of olive oil over the base. Add the onions, thyme, salt and pepper and leave to melt over a low heat, stirring occasionally.

Meanwhile, press the puff pastry or bread dough out evenly in a 20–22.5 cm (8–9 inch) square tart pan. Place a clean white cloth over it and leave to rise for about 40 minutes at room temperature

Preheat the oven to 210°C (410°F). When the onions have broken down almost to a purée, add the anchovy fillets and cook for a further 5 minutes.

Spread the onion mixture over the pastry or bread dough then bake in the preheated oven for 20 minutes.

Remove the pissaladière from the oven, leaving it turned on. Scatter the olives over the top of the onion mixture, return to the oven and continue baking for a further 5 minutes.

ABOVE: THE TERRACE OF THE L'AUBERGE RESTAURANT.

RIGHT: THE CHATEAU DE BERNE COOKERY SCHOOL.

hands or my mind. I love to show people how to prepare a meal. I want them to understand that it is not always complicated, that it is a question of instinct. Cooking with passion and with the desire to please someone is what makes the difference.'

The school offers four-day and weekend residential courses, as well as a series of cookery mornings (on Fridays and Saturdays) throughout the year, and tailor-made programmes. A typical three-day weekend course includes a visit to the bustling market at the nearby village of Lorgues, a session at an olive oil mill, lunch at a traditional local restaurant, as well as a tour of the Château de Berne's cellar and a tutored wine-tasting. The classes involve a demonstration and practical session, in turn followed by a long leisurely lunch or dinner.

On market days the afternoon is spent cooking, using the fresh produce purchased at the market in the morning, but in fact all the dishes and menus taught at the cookery school are seasonally led. Jean-Louis will tailor-make a course to suit your interests but has also devised seven from which guests can choose, covering the most popular and intriguing aspects of the local cuisine.

In Cuisine Grand-mère he teaches guests some of France's best-known traditional country dishes, as well as sharing some of his own grandmother's favourite recipes, notably her rich chocolate cake. The Provençal Cooking course includes some of the region's oldest and most popular dishes including aïoli, cassoulet, pissaladière and ratatouille. The famous Marseilles fishermen's recipe for bouillabaisse is featured in Provençal

OPPOSITE LEFT: FRESHLY PICKED ONIONS AT THE MARKET IN AIX EN PROVENCE.

OPPOSITE RIGHT: PROVENÇAL OLIVE OILS — AN ESSENTIAL INGREDIENT IN FRENCH COOKING.

WORKERS PICKING THE WINE HARVEST AT CHATEAU DE BERNE.

Fisherman's Cooking, in which visitors prepare and cook a wide variety of fresh local fish and try a range of French seafood recipes, modern and traditional.

There are two courses on cooking with olive oil, using oil straight from the estate's own groves. One focuses on olive oil's use in Provençal cuisine, with dishes incorporating aromatic wild herbs, organic vegetables and other fresh, local produce, plus Côtes de Provence wines. The other picks up on the renowned health benefits of olive oil and the Mediterranean diet, and includes traditional and modern dishes that Jean-Louis describes as being good for body and soul. Also linked to the château's own produce is Everyday Cooking with Wine, which reveals wine's role as a 'secret ingredient' in French cooking, one

that elevates everyday dishes to something special. Here Jean-Louis covers dishes such as coq au vin, boeuf bourgignon, sea bass in white wine sauce, and strawberries in red wine sauce.

If you're already familiar with classic Provençal food and are looking for something more innovative, try Jean-Louis Vosgien's Spices, Chillies and Curries programme. In his own cuisine, like many other chefs working in France at the moment, Jean-Louis is passionate about the exoticism and vibrancy that spices and fresh herbs can bring to the plate, and in this course shows how to combine them in different ways to achieve different tastes and flavours. Ginger, galangal, lime leaves, lemongrass, coriander (cilantro), basil, cardamom and saffron are amongst those used.

provence

Classes at L'Ecole de Cuisine du Château de Berne are limited to ten people, who work together in groups with Jean-Louis to produce dishes in the country-style kitchen. The auberge can accommodate many more however, so non-cooking partners are welcome, and there is plenty for them to do while you labour at the stoves, including making use of the estate's fitness studio, saunas, treatment room, tennis courts, boules pitch, mountain bikes and infinity pool. Golf and horse riding are available locally. Another treat not to be missed during your visit is one of the sessions on perfume making, with the top 'nose' from France's famous Molinard perfume house.

Book cookery courses at L'Ecole de Cuisine du Château de Berne via Gourmet on Tour (see right).

While you're in the south of France

Chef Alex Mackay, an award-winning author and former director of the cookery school at Raymond Blanc's Le Manoir aux Quat' Saisons, runs courses at Le Baou d'Infer, about 20 minutes' drive from Saint Tropez. There is a maximum class size of six to optimise personal attention. Visit www.lebaou.com for details.
At the Hostellerie Bérard, a cluster of beautifully restored old buildings in the magnificent Provençal village of La Cadière d'Azur near Cassis, French Master Chef René Bérard leads classes in Provencal cooking using herbs and vegetables from the garden. See www.hotel-berard.com.

Other courses in France

Day courses including:
Food Lovers Tour Côte d'Azur – discover the food of southern France with hands-on cooking and a walking tour. No accommodation included.

Five-day courses including:
Passport to Provence – this course is held in a superb old house with its own herb-and-vegetable garden. Participants visit local markets and local vineyards, all enhanced by the fascinating story of Provence. Accommodation included.

Contact: Gourmet on Tour
Berkeley Square House
2F Berkeley Square
Mayfair
London W1J 6BD
Tel UK +44 (0)2 7396 5550
Fax UK +44 (0)2 7900 1527
Tel US 1 800 504 9842
Fax US 1 800 886 2229
www.gourmetontour.com

Rosemary Barron's Greece,
Santorini, Greece

Even Greek people are envious when they find you plan to visit Santorini. It is considered one of the loveliest and most stylish islands in the Mediterranean. Author and teacher Rosemary Barron, who is board director of the International Association of Culinary Professionals, has been running programmes on the island for several years. Prior to that, in the 1980s, she ran a renowned cookery school on Crete, the first to focus on the cultural aspects of Greek food. This hands-on experience, plus her acute fascination with history and the health aspects of ingredients, guarantees an absorbing introduction to all that is good in Greek cuisine.

It's the typically Greek peasant-style pots and plates that really irritate Rosemary Barron. Not here on Santorini, but in books, magazines and travel literature published around the world. 'Santorini is a very sophisticated and glamorous island, one of the most expensive in the Mediterranean,' she says indignantly. 'Much as I love the earthy homeliness of Greek food, it does aggravate me that our food and wine are always shown in rustic pottery.'

Selene, the beautiful restaurant in which she usually conducts her classes on Santorini, is certainly stylish enough to be found in New York. Greek wines are now winning medals on the world stage, 'and still it's peasant pots shown in the pictures.' Now running classes on Santorini for the fourth year, Rosemary admits her course has evolved to focus less on cooking, more on the antiquity of Greek food. 'There is less chopping of onions,' she says. 'In fact, there is no chopping of onions. It's very much more about sampling, experiencing and working things out for yourself. We use history to follow the thread of food through the ages, from classical Greece to modern Greek cuisine. Afterwards, people find they can travel through Greece with a very good knowledge of what's what.'

THE STUNNING SIGHT OF SANTORINI'S ROOF TOPS.

The historical focus is less surprising when you learn that Rosemary first came to Greece in the late 1960s when she was an archaeology student. Although she subsequently decided to become a school teacher instead, she remained interested in the ancient culture. 'Greek food has been around a long time,' she says, 'and classical Greece was the first time food was intellectualized. Threads from those days live on in modern Greek cuisine.'

Enhancing the interest further is the fact that food's role in well-being was clocked here long before the World Health Organization started promoting the Mediterranean diet. 'Hippocrates was the father of modern medicine and performed his medicine through food,' says Rosemary. 'He understood food's relationship to health and medicine and that lives on here. Also Greece has for many centuries been a poor country and therefore did not have the opportunity to lose its traditional cuisine as we have in English-speaking countries. Some of the very best foods native to the eastern Mediterranean have been proven to be crawling with nutrients — think of rocket, purslane, watercress. Greek oregano, which is different from the Italian, is very high in antioxidants and the Greeks use it by the handful, yet no one else does.'

Although not vegetarian, Greek cuisine is a good area of study for those people who do not like eating a lot of meat. 'Greece has the most fasts of any culture,' adds Rosemary. 'They are strict and long.'

FILO PIES FILLED WITH SPINACH, RED PEPPER, LEEKS HERBS AND LEMON, ONE OF ROSEMARY'S SPECIALITIES.

Sweet-Savoury Honey Pears

SERVES 6

4 tablespoons red-wine vinegar

125 ml (4 fl oz) (½ cup) mild-flavored honey
   such as wild flower or blossom

900 ml (1½ pints) (4 cups) water

2 bay leaves

10 sprigs of thyme

6 small, firm pears

FOR SERVING

kamaiki (thick cream) or strained yoghurt

12 walnuts, shelled

'The skills of the chefs of Greek antiquity inspired this simple and elegant dessert,' says Rosemary. 'Walnuts, rich yoghurt, thyme, cinnamon, vinegar and honey were some of their favourite ingredients, and they were said to have used over twenty varieties of pear.'

Combine the vinegar, honey, water, bay leaves, and 4 sprigs of thyme in a deep non-reactive saucepan, just large enough to hold the pears in a single layer. Place over a low heat and bring gently to the boil.

Peel the pears, leaving the stems intact and reserving the peel. Add the pears and peel to the pan, then if needed, add more water — enough to cover the pears. Bring to a simmer and cook uncovered for 20 minutes, or until the pears begin to turn translucent.

Using a slotted spoon, remove the pears from the pan and arrange in a dish. Raise the heat under the pan and boil until the cooking liquid becomes syrupy, for about 25 minutes. Strain the syrup over the pears and discard the peel and herbs. Set aside to cool.

To serve, arrange the pears on six small plates and spoon over most of the syrup. Arrange a spoonful of kamaiki or yoghurt alongside each pear and drizzle with the remaining syrup. Garnish with the walnuts and the rest of the thyme sprigs.

She reels off the cuisine's other attributes: 'It's a very practical cuisine. Everything is eaten, including the garnishes. It has many inexpensive dishes that nevertheless have complex flavours. It's colourful and although it can be labour-intensive, many dishes can be made the day before serving.'

Still not convinced you should be interested? The sceptical view of Greek food has taken a long time to dissipate, even with the fashionable Mediterranean cooking. Indeed, one of the reasons Rosemary began cooking in Greece in the 1980s was because people kept asking her what it was about the country that attracted her. Prior to that she had spent a few years in London teaching high

school, then moved to the U.S.A. where she met Chuck Williams. He invited her to travel between the Williams-Sonoma stores giving cooking classes to show customers how to use the kitchen equipment on sale. She wound up living in San Francisco for 12 years and still makes many appearances in the U.S.A., giving classes at Williams Sonoma, Sur La Table, private cooking schools, community education facilities, and (a favourite) at the Central Market Stores in Texas.

'Being a school teacher is very different from being a cookery teacher,' says Rosemary. 'Children tend not to want to come to school whereas people do want to come to cookery school. But high

school is an excellent grounding. You become organized. You get your timing right (that is almost essential) and it teaches you how to control and use your voice.' A typical week-long course with Rosemary on Santorini starts with a Monday arrival and ends the following Sunday when guests leave. In between there are four days of workshops and tastings, with plenty of time for culture, tours, walks and shopping worked into the schedule. Rosemary gives most of the workshops herself but brings in local experts Evelyn Volika and George Hatziannakis for the session on traditional foods and ingredients of the Cycladic Islands. This is followed by a tasting of around ten artisan-produced cheeses only

available locally. On Wednesday Rosemary leads a workshop on Greek herbs, flavours and cooking techniques, covering the wide range of fresh leaves that are used in copious quantities in Greek cooking: flat leaf parsley, dill, fennel, coriander (cilantro), thyme, marjoram, lemon balm and sweet geranium. The session also takes in the use of dried varieties such as rigani, bay, thyme, sage, rosemary and marjoram. There is a private tour of the Sigalas Winery with local mezze to sample, and a session focusing exclusively on horta and other seasonal Greek foods.

Meals with wines are all included, some at Selene and others at various local tavernas. Most guests want comfortable pension-style rooms, not too expensive, but should you require something grander, it can be easily arranged. Rosemary offers tailor-made courses too, and visitors are not restricted to Santorini, beautiful though it may be. She is also an expert on Crete and the Peloponnese and can organize food-related trips all over Greece, working in as many cultural aspects (such as music) as required. A minimum stay would sensibly be for four days. Travel to Santorini typically requires taking a connecting flight from Athens, but if you're prepared to take a bus trip across the city, the early morning ferry is one of the most inspiring ways to arrive.

Ancient Wisdom, Modern Tables is currently the only course offered by Rosemary between May and October, annually.
Includes six days of cookery workshops, tastings of wine, olive oils and cheeses, traditional meals and guided tours of the local area. A choice of accommodation is included.

Contact: Rosemary Barron
12 Centenary Way
Cheddar
Somerset
BS27 3DG
UK
Tel and fax: +44 (0)1934 741030
www.rosemarybarronsgreece.com

India on the Menu, Goa, India

Most people come to Goa on the west coast of India for the heat of the beach, not the heat of the kitchen, but this course allows visitors to combine the two in a holiday that is both fun and educational. Every student prepares their own dishes from scratch, however you don't have to be an experienced cook to participate, simply someone who loves curry. Within a day you are likely to find that you (yes, you) can produce better food than your neighbourhood Indian takeaway restaurant, and that it can be very easy to do so. Not only are many of the ingredients easy to get hold of outside India these days, but there is also a core group from which a fascinating variety of dishes can be made. Before long you will be using them without the need to refer to a recipe, because that's one of the other things this carefully conceived course has been designed to do: free participants from slavishly following printed instructions. They don't do it in India, why should you?

Climbing the stairs to this fourth-floor cooking school is aerobically challenging, especially in the intense heat of Goa's tropical climate, but once there, the effort is rewarded. The high position offers views out over the distant trees and the open covered terrace allows the unfettered flow of cooling breezes from the nearby sea. Below, emerging from powdery red soil, are straggly trees of mango, banana, custard apple and almond.

In this relaxed and rustic setting, Priya Gogte and Judy Cardozo provide visitors with a comprehensive introductory course on the diverse intricacies of Indian cuisine. Sensibly, their programme has been designed to fit neatly into a beach holiday. Over the course of a week,

guests take three hands-on cooking classes (one on southern cuisine, one on northern and a third highlighting interesting regional dishes). Guests also visit Mapusa market, the largest in northern Goa. There is plenty of time in the afternoon and on alternate days for sun-bathing and swimming.

When it comes to cooking, however, the approach is enjoyably serious. Priya, an experienced chef and restaurateur, is adamant that everyone on the course should prepare the dishes from scratch. 'If people cook, they remember. If I'm demonstrating you might as well be watching it on television,' she explains. 'The aim is that people can go home and cook an Indian meal without looking at a

OPPOSITE: SPICES ARE NOT JUST FLAVOURINGS; THEY ARE CONSIDERED HEALTH-PROMOTING TOO.

RIGHT: ACCOMMODATION AT THE TAJ VILLAGE RESORT.

Goan Fish Curry

Goans say that without a portion of this delicious dish, they don't enjoy their meal. The rich orange colour of a true Goan fish curry may surprise those who've been enjoying the yellowy-beige dish of that name from supermarket chiller cabinets. However there are numerous fresh red chillies in the spice paste, so it is very much a natural colour. Including raw rice in the paste helps to thicken the curry, and gives it a pleasantly different texture from the other saucy dishes served as part of a meal. Be sure not to let the coconut milk boil once you have added it to the pan.

SERVES 4

FOR THE SPICE PASTE

8–10 fresh red chillies

1 garlic clove

1 teaspoon plain white rice

1 tablespoon ground coriander

½ tablespoon ground cumin

½ teaspoon turmeric

a small ball of tamarind

4 tablespoons hot water

500 g (1 lb) king fish or other fleshy,
    firm fish (such as tuna)

salt

2 tablespoons neutral-flavoured vegetable oil

1 onion, finely chopped

675 ml (1 pint 3 fl oz) (3 scant cups) thick
    coconut milk

2 fresh green chillies

To make the spice paste, combine the red chillies, garlic, rice, coriander, cumin and turmeric in a small blender or spice mill and grind to a fine paste. Set aside.

Break up the tamarind and place in a heatproof bowl. Cover with 4 tablespoons of hot water. Stir a little, using a metal teaspoon, pressing the tamarind against the side of the bowl to encourage it to break down. Set aside to soak.

Cut the fish into generous bite-sized pieces and salt them lightly. Set aside.

Heat the oil in a kadai, small wok or medium saucepan. Add the chopped onion and fry over a medium heat until the onion is pale yellow, stirring often to prevent catching and burning. Add the spice paste and fry lightly for about 3 minutes, stirring often.

Pour in the coconut milk and stir to combine thoroughly. Allow the mixture to come to a gentle simmer but don't let it boil hard or the coconut milk will split. As soon as the sauce mixture is bubbling, reduce the heat to low.

Meanwhile, stir the tamarind again and press the brown liquid through a small sieve into a little dish, to remove the seeds and strings from the fruit.

Add the fish to the pan and cook gently until the sauce begins to come to a simmer again. Stir in the tamarind liquid. Cut a slit lengthways in each of the green chillies and add them to the pan, then add salt to taste. Remove from the heat and serve with rice.

OPPOSITE: LUNCH SERVED IN A THALI (A SMALL
SELECTION OF DIFFERENT DISHES) ON THE TERRACE.

RIGHT: DISHES SUCH AS PALAK PANEER (CREAMY
SPINACH CURRY), OFTEN SERVED WITH NAAN (INDIAN
FLATBREAD), ARE TAKEN FROM ALL OVER INDIA,
NOT JUST GOA.

recipe and without having to hunt down special ingredients. If the food is easy to cook, people will make it again and again, whereas they won't make complicated dishes at home more than once or twice, if at all.'

She passes around two flow-charts, one for north Indian cuisine and one for the south. They clearly show how formulaic even the most complex-tasting curries can be. 'It may be that the cook slices instead of dices the onions, or uses tamarind as a souring agent in place of lime, yoghurt or vinegar, but still there is this basic order of cooking, a simple yet careful system,' says Priya. 'Don't get hung up on what is

and what isn't available, or whether it's fresh or dried. The water's different from one place to another anyway, and that will affect the result, so don't worry.'

Although a recipe book is provided for each student, Priya wants to give students the confidence to cook instinctively, not make them feel trapped by instructions and measuring spoons. 'Nobody gives accurate measurements here in India because people don't use them. If you ask, they say "just use your judgement". You don't get the exact same result every single time, but that is the key to Indian cooking: it is not the same every time. We call it "flavour of the hand".'

Her explanations of regional variations and historical trends are enhanced by pointing to a large map of the subcontinent on the kitchen wall. 'A lot of the "northern cuisine" served in restaurants is actually food of the north-west frontier which is influenced by Iran and Afghanistan. Kashmiri cuisine in particular is very similar to that of Iran and Afghanistan. It's elaborate. Southern Indian food is simpler and less flashy, like the people. Their language is less flowery, they are more reserved, and this shows in the cuisine.'

The day's menu is written on a blackboard. Guests work all morning preparing several dishes that together comprise a balanced

OPPOSITE LEFT: GRINDING CHILLIES FOR A SPICE PASTE.

OPPOSITE RIGHT: MAPSUA HAS THE AREA'S MOST
BUSTLING AND AUTHENTIC MARKET.

FRESHLY CAUGHT LOCAL FISH ARE A MAINSTAY OF THE
GOAN (AND TOURISTIC) DIET.

Indian meal that is served on the terrace for lunch. Throughout the sessions Priya explains the hows and whys of ingredient preparation. She shows us how to run our fingers along a branch of curry leaves to quickly remove them from the stem and release their nutty fragrance, and how to temper the heat of fresh chilli by cutting a slit and using it whole rather than minced. 'When it's cooked and on the plate, you can squeeze it to release more chilli flavour if you want it,' she advises.

In Priya's teaching kitchen, India's distinctive round spice box becomes a practical tool rather than a trendy item from a pretentious kitchenware catalogue. 'The spice box is one of the keys to making Indian food regularly,' she advises. 'The spices all have to go in the pan in rapid succession. You can't hold four spice jars in one hand and open them up – they'll burn before they're all added. Always hold the spice box steady and straight and use the same spoon to add each of the spices.'

There are two schools of thought on correct cooking of spices. One is to heat the oil first and throw in the spices so that they start to pop immediately. The second, which Priya favours, is to add the spices to the cold oil in the pan and heat them until they pop. 'Some believe the second way releases more flavour, but it also gives you more control over the cooking

and the spices are less likely to burn,' she rationalises.

Much insight is given into the nutritional properties associated with ingredients in India, though it's a complex subject that could take years to fathom. Saffron is used in rice puddings in the north of the country to produce heat in the body, whereas southerners favour cardamom in the same dish for its cooling qualities. Nutmeg induces grogginess, so is only used for evening meals or if an afternoon siesta is planned. Cumin and aniseed aid digestion. There is a fascinating tradition of frugality too: 'We believe it is a sin to throw food out,' says Priya. 'We use fish heads to make curry, and fry the fillets to serve them separately. Even cauliflower stalk will be used in a dish and, actually, is considered the most prized part.'

The course has been devised so that people can participate no matter where they are staying locally. However tour operator On the Go will arrange accommodation at the prestigious Taj Holiday Village, about ten minutes' drive from Priya's restaurant. A key advantage of staying here is the opportunity to dine at the Beach House, whose executive chef Urbano do Rego is India's most respected authority on Goan cuisine, and one of Priya's former teachers. Now, however, the student has become an authority in her own way too.

This week-long cookery course is currently the only course offered by On The Go. Includes four hands-on cookery classes where you will learn to make aromatic rice and vegetarian, chicken, fish and seafood curries. Also includes visits to local markets and advice on spices and kitchen equipment. Accommodation packages are optional.

Contact: On the Go
68 North End Road
West Kensington
London W14 9EP
Tel +44 (0)20 7371 1113
Fax +44 (0)20 7471 6414
www.onthegotours.com

Ballymaloe Cookery School, Cork, Ireland

Housed in an old apple barn on an historic property, the Ballymaloe Cookery School is one of Ireland's most famous culinary institutions, owned by award-winning cookery writer and tv-chef Darina Allen. Since opening the school in 1983, she has gradually developed the curriculum to incorporate a strong emphasis on fresh local produce and organic food production, quite different from other professional cooking schools around the world. Neither do you need to be an aspiring or established chef to attend — the school offers various short courses from half a day to five days long, to inspire home cooks and absolute beginners.

Surely not all Irish people want to travel to Paris or London to learn how to cook. That was Darina Allen's train of thought in the early 1980s when the downturn in the farming business grew progressively worse and prompted a reassessment of how she and husband Tim should be earning a living. 'At that time people went to the Cordon Bleu in Paris or London and I thought a residential cooking school was needed in Ireland,' she explains.

Her instinct was right and for many years now Ballymaloe Cookery School has been regarded as a leading teaching centre for professional cooks, not just in Ireland, but around the world. Much of the business still focuses on three-month certificate programmes run for people who eventually want to earn money from their cooking. However Ballymaloe's unique point of difference from other professional certificate courses is that the school is run from Darina and Tim's organic farm, with its own beef cattle, happy free-range pigs, chickens,

beehives, herb, fruit and vegetable gardens, and the classes make full use of the ingredients.

'Good food starts in the good earth,' says Darina, who admits she is passionate about soil fertility. 'Scraps from the cookery school go to the hens. We have a couple of Jersey cows and students can milk the cows if they want to, and learn how to make yogurt and cream. They meet the farm manager; they go out with the gardeners. They learn how to sow seeds and, during the course, grow their own plants from seed, which not only gives them a tremendous amount of satisfaction but an understanding of the holistic nature of food.'

Ballymaloe Cookery School's gardens have become a visitor attraction in their own right and are open to the public daily from Easter to September. The school also runs a variety of gardening courses including Organic Gardening and Grow Your Own Vegetables with specialist

THE HERB GARDEN AT BALLYMALOE COOKERY SCHOOL

ABOVE: SALAD MADE FROM LEAVES AND FLOWERS PICKED FROM THEIR OWN GARDEN.

Roscommon Rhubarb Pie

'Everyone adores this delectable tart,' says Darina. 'It's an adaptation of a traditional recipe that was originally cooked in a bastable (a three-legged iron pot) over the open fire. We use a heavy stainless steel sauté pan which works very well. If you don't have a suitable pan, parcook the rhubarb slightly first.' For a variation, try adding a couple of teaspoons of freshly grated ginger to the rhubarb.

SERVES 8–10

1 kg (2 lb) red rhubarb
250–275 g (8–9 oz) (1¼–1⅓ cups) granulated sugar, plus extra for sprinkling
a little beaten egg mixed with water
soft brown sugar, to serve
cream, to serve

FOR THE TOPPING
300 g (10 oz) (scant 2 cups) flour
2 tablespoons caster (superfine) sugar
1 heaped teaspoon baking powder
a pinch of salt
50 g (2 oz) butter
175ml (6 fl oz) (¾ cup) full cream milk
1 egg

Preheat the oven to 230°C (450°F) Gas Mark 8. Trim the rhubarb, wipe with a damp cloth and cut into pieces about 2.5 cm (1 inch) in length. Put into the base of a 23 x 5 cm (9 x 2 inch) round tin or ovenproof sauté pan and sprinkle with the sugar. Place over a low heat on the stove while you make the dough topping.

Sieve the flour, caster sugar, baking powder and salt into a mixing bowl. Cut the butter into cubes and rub them into the dry ingredients until the mixture resembles coarse breadcrumbs.

Combine the milk and egg in a measuring jug and whisk together. Make a well in the centre of the flour mixture, pour in the liquid all at once, and mix to a soft dough.

Turn the dough out onto a floured surface and roll into a 23 cm (9 inch) round about 2.5 cm (1 inch) thick. Place the dough on top of the rhubarb and tuck in the edges neatly. Brush with a little egg wash and sprinkle with granulated sugar.

Bake for 15 minutes, then reduce the oven temperature to 180°C (350°F) Gas Mark 4 and continue baking for a further 30 minutes or so, until the top of the pie is crusty and golden and the rhubarb underneath is soft and juicy.

Remove the pie from the oven and allow it to sit for a few minutes. Put a warm plate over the top of the pan or tin and invert it onto the plate, being careful of the hot cooking juices. Serve warm with soft brown sugar and cream.

Susan Turner. Boasting more than 70 different species, the herb garden is often thought by visitors to be old but was created just nine years ago. The surrounding beech hedges create a microclimate in which tender herbs, like lemon verbena, thrive. Two mint beds feature several varieties including Moroccan, ginger, Bowles' mint, apple, spearmint and chocolate mint. Some of the plants, such as globe artichokes, lovage, cardoons and angelica, bring an architectural quality to the display.

The herb garden's layout is both beautiful and practical, so that it is easy to harvest. Every morning, one of the gardeners, together with a cookery student, will pick herbs for use in the school. They also harvest purslane, salad burnet, sorrel, golden marjoram and edible flowers for the green salad that is prepared each day for lunch in the cookery school in the Garden Café. Spring brings edible wild garlic flowers, while in the summer months nasturtiums, chive flowers, borage and calendula are used.

The fruit garden, adjacent to the converted apple barn that now houses the school, features berries of many species, shape and size: black and white mulberries, various currants and gooseberries, red and golden raspberries, tayberries, boysenberries, strawberries, and American cranberries and blueberries. There are pears, plums and greengages, crab apples, quinces, almond and olive trees. 'One surprising success has been the

Asian pear or nashi tree,' says Darina. 'The trees have produced excellent, crisp fruits that are apple-like with a heavy russet.' Some old apple varieties, including Irish Peach, Egremont Russet, Pitmaston Pineapple and Arthur Turner, were added to the collection in 1994 and are being trained over tall arches. The violet flowers, which are at their most abundant in winter and early spring, are crystallized and used to decorate desserts and cakes, while elderflowers are turned into cool seasonal drinks.

A screen of trees with a wicket gate to exclude the flock of free-range hens, hides the potager or vegetable garden. It is laid out in a series of diamonds and squares with herringbone paths of old brick, laid by a local craftsman. While it provides fresh and full-flavoured organic produce for the school, it has also been designed to show that vegetables can be ornamental, colourful and fragrant. A couple of scarecrows stand guarding the crops, which include sea kale, squash, chillies, oriental vegetables, asparagus,

ABOVE: DARINA ALLEN (CENTRE) TEACHING.

ruby chard and a variety of lettuces
and other salad leaves. There is also a
collection of old potato varieties, including
Pink Fir Apple and Sharps Express.

Even with this incredible bounty on the
doorstep, Darina has always been an
enthusiastic collector of foods that grow
wild in the Irish countryside too. She calls
them 'natural treasures that taste superb'
and leads a one-day Foraging course —
the morning devoted to hunting the
ingredients, and the afternoon spent
back at the school using them to best
advantage. Fruit such as elderberries and
crab apples are turned into jellies, nettles
and wild watercress are made into soup,
rosehips into delicious healthy syrup,
carageen moss into puddings, comfrey
into fritters. 'These days, trend-setting
chefs are employing foragers to help give

STUDENTS GET INVOLVED ON THE FARM IN ORDER TO
UNDERSTAND THE HOLISTIC NATURE OF GOOD FOOD.

their cooking an edge, so the time is ripe for a new appreciation of the good things we take so much for granted in our fields and hedgerows,' says Darina.

Another intriguing course for travellers is Irish Traditional Food and Music, which runs for two and a half days. In it, Darina, who wrote the award-winning book *Irish Traditional Cooking*, covers classic recipes such as soda bread, colcannon, Irish stew, Dingle pie, Ulster champ and Roscommon rhubarb tart. 'There's more to Irish food than corned beef and cabbage,' she says. 'Guests learn about our traditional food culture and in the evenings we get together in local pubs for traditional music and craic.'

The five-day intensive courses are designed to transform complete beginners into home cooks who can prepare delicious meals and entertain with panache. Alternatively, people can drop in for half-day demonstrations, sitting in on classes held for the professional certificate course.

There is a limited amount of accommodation at the cookery school, where guests stay in converted l8th century farm buildings. Two miles away is Ballymaloe House, the country house hotel owned by Darina's mother, Myrtle Allen, another charming place to stay.

Courses currently available

One day courses including:
Cooking for One or Two – Cooking is sometimes tricky to adapt for one or two; this course will cover recipes for starters, main courses and puddings and provide basic techniques that can be adapted in a variety of ways.

Five-day courses including:
Intensive Introductory Course – Perfect for those who want to learn the basics quickly. With six demonstrations, and four hands-on sessions, this course teaches all the essential skills – making breads, soups, pâtés, roasts, vegetable dishes, desserts, pastry – right through to jam and biscuits.

Contact: Ballymaloe Cookery School
Shanagarry
Midelton
County Cork, Ireland
Tel: +353 (0)21 4646 785
Fax:+353 (0)21 4646 909
www.cookingisfun.ie

Diane Seed's Roman Kitchen, Rome, Italy

One of Rome's most prestigious palazzos, the stunning Palazzo Doria Pamphili houses an art gallery featuring the Doria Pamphili family's collection of paintings, as well as the cooking school run by former academic and Italian food authority Diane Seed. Through the round window of her top floor kitchen, guests can look out over the Piazza Venezia, down to the Forum and the Colosseum. The back terrace affords a view of the dome of St. Peter's. Courses run for the best part of a week — from Sunday evening until the following Friday — with a maximum of 12 participants. The style is relaxed, informal and conversational. You can do hands-on cooking, or sit back and watch if preferred. Most guests choose a mixture of both. Diane maintains a careful balance between food for dinner parties and interesting quick dishes to prepare for midweek suppers, so you'll be impressing friends and family with the things you've learned on this course on a regular basis for years to come.

Rome's Testaccio market is, like many European markets, situated where the city's old slaughterhouse used to be. It has been dismissed by some as shabby, not a place to linger, but such descriptions make Diane Seed rather indignant. 'I've been lingering here for years,' she jokes, 'and I still find it very exciting.'

It is just one of the markets visited during her week-long cooking courses. Diane believes Rome is the ideal city in which to have an introduction to Italian cooking. 'All roads lead to Rome, so all the produce is here. There's ancient Rome, fashionable Rome and Vatican Rome — something for everyone,' she says.

The author of several best-selling cookbooks, including *The Top 100 Pasta Sauces*, Diane has lived in the city for over thirty years but hails from London, England. She jokes that she fell in love with an Italian man, then fell in love with Italy, then fell in love with Italian food. 'I've been very privileged,' she says. 'I was a reluctant transfer, I thought I

would miss London too much.' These days, after many trips abroad, Diane finds that in many respects she still feels terribly English, but when it comes to food she is 100 per cent Italian. Being an expatriate has helped rather than hindered. It's opened doors. Italian people will reveal recipes to her that they would never reveal to another Italian person.

Typical classes are run from Monday to Thursday, 10.30 am to 2 pm, but the course kicks off on Sunday evening where you are a guest for dinner in Diane's private apartment. It's a clever ice-breaker, so that everyone feels comfortable when classes start on Monday, and by Tuesday's session they've started bonding. Having afternoons and evenings free makes the course an ideal mix of food and travel and provides an opportunity for people who want to spend some time exploring Rome, and also for those who have a non-cooking partner. It's also a comfortable option for singles who can go off and do their own thing.

THE IMPRESSIVE TREVI FOUNTAIN IN PIAZZA NAVONA IN THE HEART OF ROME.

BUYING FRESH INGREDIENTS FROM THE LOCAL MARKETS.

The hands-on portion of the course is very Italian. Guests cook together and talk as they prepare the dishes. It doesn't matter that some people in the group are only just learning to cook while others may be professionals. 'I find it always works, whatever the mix of people, and at the end of each day everyone can replicate the four dishes we've cooked, even if they are beginners.' However, Diane never tells people in advance what dishes they're going to be making during the classes. 'I don't think you can,' she says simply. 'We go to the market and see what's available. If something looks irresistible, we buy it and squeeze it into the class. Food is very seasonal here. For example, this year spring vegetables came much earlier than usual, so of course we used them.'

Nearest to the palazzo is the Campo de' Fiori, a flower, food, and vegetable market since the Middle Ages. It used to be the place to come to watch executions, now it's a great place to shop and enjoy a cappuccino. 'Markets in Rome are going to dwindle and dwindle,' says Diane reflectively. 'The rents charged by the councils are so high. Old people die out and the youngsters don't want to take over. Every year there are fewer stalls. But this one is different from any other. It's moved with the times and is fighting back.'

Spring Vegetable Lasagne

Diane loves to make this dish, also known as lasagne primavera, when the first spring vegetables appear in the market. The béchamel sauce is made fragrant with fresh basil leaves. If you are using broad beans, remove the outer skins after boiling to reveal the pretty, bright-green inner bean.

SERVES 6

500 g (1 lb) small, tender courgettes (zucchini)

a splash of olive oil

12 sheets white lasagne

18 spears green asparagus

200 g (7 oz) (1 ⅓ cups) shelled peas or very small broad beans

200 g (7 oz) thin green beans

125 g (4 oz) (scant 1 cup) freshly grated Parmesan cheese

1 small, fresh mozzarella cheese, about 125 g (4½ oz)

1–2 tablespoons butter

FOR THE BECHAMEL SAUCE

55 g (2 oz) (½ stick) butter

55 g (2 oz) (⅓ cup) flour

1 litre (1¾ pints) (4¼ cups) milk

a little grated nutmeg

salt and freshly ground black pepper

20 basil leaves

Bring a large pan of salted water to the boil. Meanwhile, cut the courgettes into thin discs. Get ready a large bowl of cold water to refresh the cooked pasta, and spread out some clean kitchen towels to dry it.

Add a little olive oil to the boiling water to prevent the pasta sticking, then cook the pasta sheets two at a time. After a few minutes, lift out the pasta with a slotted spoon and plunge it into the bowl of cold water. Remove from the cold water and spread out on the kitchen towels to dry. Do not put the pasta sheets on top of each other or they will stick together. Repeat until all the pasta sheets are cooked.

To make the béchamel sauce, melt the butter in a saucepan. Whisk in the flour and cook for 1 minute with the mixture bubbling. Remove the saucepan from the heat and slowly add the milk a little at a time, stirring constantly with a wooden spoon or whisk. Ensure all the milk is incorporated into the sauce before you add any more. Return the pan to the heat and bring to a boil, stirring constantly until the sauce thickens.

Season the béchamel to taste with grated nutmeg, salt and pepper, then remove from the heat and allow to cool. Combine the bechamel and basil leaves in a food processor or blender and whizz to give a smooth, pale green sauce.

Cook the vegetables separately in a pan of boiling, salted water fitted with a blanching basket so that the cooked vegetables are easy to remove from the pan before adding the next batch. The vegetables should be slightly underdone.

Preheat the oven to 200°C (400°F) Gas Mark 6. Butter a rectangular oven dish and coat the base with a thin layer of sauce. Line with three slightly overlapping pasta sheets, spooning a little sauce at the pasta seams. Arrange a sprinkling of vegetables over the sheets, dust with a little Parmesan cheese and black pepper and then spoon over some more sauce. Build up the layers in this way, reserving some good-looking vegetables for decoration.

When you have added the final layer of pasta sheets, thinly slice the mozzarella and arrange it evenly over the top. Decorate with the reserved vegetables. Add a light sprinkling of Parmesan, dot the surface with a little butter, and bake the lasagne in the preheated oven for about 20 minutes.

A TYPICAL ITALIAN CAFÉ.

OPPOSITE: PARKED MOPEDS ARE A COMMON SIGHT
LINING THE STREETS OF ROME.

She buys raspberries for a panna cotta from a man known as the Bulgari of greengrocers. 'They have special things here, such beautiful produce, I always buy too much,' says Diane. That's not a problem for this vendor, who has motorbikes ready to carry the chosen goods back to his customers' kitchens.

Recipes for the classes are drawn from all over Italy. In some respects Rome doesn't have much going for it, gastronomically speaking. 'It's been called a city of priests and politicians,' Diane admits. Some of the most traditional dishes are based on animal intestines, feet, heads, tails — even Romans don't particularly want to eat them nowadays. There is a luscious, and

delightfully simple, Roman dish of pasta, pecorino romano cheese and pepper. Lamb in the huntsman's style is cooked with masses of rosemary, garlic and vinegar. Artichoke dishes are associated with the city too, and there is an interesting history of Jewish cuisine. 'They used a lot of anchovy because in the past they could not have prosciutto,' Diane explains, so courgette (zucchini) flowers would be stuffed with mozarella and anchovies, and then deep-fried in a yeasted batter.

She has a particular interest in Monzù cuisine, the dishes that evolved when the great aristocratic families of Italy employed French chefs — and couldn't

pronounce the word monsieur. This trend resulted in French recipes and techniques being applied to Italian ingredients, and the creation of elaborate dishes suitable for entertaining.

People often say it's the stories she tells that makes Diane's classes so special but, to her, it's the wonderful Italian food that's the linchpin. Nevertheless she does like to discover, and reveal, the story behind each of the dishes. 'It sounds more pretentious than it is,' she says in typically self-effacing style, 'but I do like to look at social history through food.'

She never planned to become a top-selling cookery author, and has never

trained at a culinary school. 'I hate measuring. I always give people recipes in class, but I can't actually measure while I'm cooking because it seems to artificial.' Yet she felt inspired to start leading cookery classes because, as a former teacher of English literature, she missed the degree of contact with people that teaching requires.

Clients often ask why she doesn't open a school in Tuscany, the region everyone seems to want to visit. 'Actually, I don't like the Tuscan dishes so much. My big love is the South. Puglia is one of the first places I ever gave classes and it is a region people would struggle to discover by themselves.' Diane still runs classes

there, and on the Amalfi coast. Some people have started running cookery courses just because they have a romantic property that they don't know what to do with. Diane is different. 'I want people to share the passion that I have. I've been very privileged.'

Courses currently include

Rome – A week spent at Diane's Roman kitchen includes cooking demonstrations, hands-on cookery lessons, visits to local food markets and speciality shops. No accommodation included

Amalfi Coast – Based in Sant' Agata, hands-on cooking lessons explore pasta, vegetables and fish. Includes demonstrations of limoncello (lemon liqueur) and mozzarella making. Accommodation included.

Puglia – Staying in a 16th-century farmhouse, this week-long course involves five cooking lessons, visits to local food and olive oil producers and tours around local towns. Accommodation included.

Contact: Diane Seed's Roman Kitchen
Via del Plebiscito, 112
Roma 00186
Tel. +39 06 6797103
Fax +39 06 6797109
www.italiangourmet.com

The Coselli School of Tuscan Cuisine, Tuscany, Italy

A row of large terracotta pots trailing with heavy, fragrant lemons greets visitors to this idyllic, aristocratic estate in a tiny rural hamlet in central Italy. Here, during the 15th century, the most important families of the area created a modern farming system that saw the land divided up as it is today. However, in the 21st century, you don't have to be an Italian nobleman to enjoy the pleasures of Borgo Bernardini, the estate within the village of Coselli at which the Coselli School of Tuscan Cuisine is run. Amidst grand cypress and platano trees, surrounded by olive groves and peach orchards, the renovated estate buildings provide vibrantly decorated rooms that are both luxurious and simple, with intimate, shutter-framed views over the serene gardens and courtyards. Bedside tables and windows are swathed in rich fabrics. Even the billiard table has been vividly painted and stencilled. Yet the overall effect is relaxing. Like many country estates, day-to-day life at Borgo Bernardini is not intimidatingly formal but revolves around a warmly spacious, welcoming kitchen.

Springtime in Tuscany. The vivid green and purple artichokes from Morellino are nearing the end of their season, but any sense of disappointment in that respect is tempered by the arrival of the thin, knobbly strands of wild asparagus.

Chef Valter Roman places a large, straggly bunch on the spacious stainless steel worktop alongside a neat parcel of the more familiar cultivated asparagus to illustrate the differences. Today we are making wild asparagus ravioli with a truffle butter sauce and, as we start preparing the filling, it is easy to see why someone once thought cultivated asparagus a good idea. There's no regularity to the wild variety. The coarse bases sometimes extend more than halfway up the stems, there are soft dark, dank patches that also need to be discarded, and the thin bendy filaments seem to want to form a crazy tangle that to unpractised and hesitant fingers triples, maybe quadruples, the preparation time. But when they are finally tamed into orderly rows, chopped small, sautéed with spring onion and stirred into a creamy paste of ricotta, Parmesan and parsley, the flavour is – oh! – magnificent.

LEFT: LUCCA, A TEN MINUTE DRIVE FROM COSELLI, IS KNOWN AS THE CITY OF A HUNDRED CHURCHES.

RIGHT: BORGO BERNARDINI'S PRISTINE ORNAMENTAL GARDENS.

Ribollita

Tuscany's famous soup of black cabbage, beans and bread is so thick that on the day after serving, the leftovers can be sliced and fried to make a tasty breakfast. This recipe is one of several classic dishes of the area that frugally incorporate stale bread.

SERVES 8

250 g (8 oz) (1½ cups) dried borlotti beans, or a mixture of borlotti and cannellini beans
2 celery sticks
2 carrots
180 ml (6 fl oz) (¾ cup) extra-virgin olive oil
2 garlic cloves
a few fresh sage leaves
400 g (13 oz) black cabbage, (cavalonero) or curly kale
1 onion
2 courgettes (zucchini)
a few thin slices of day-old country bread
50 g (2 oz) (½ cup) grated Parmigiano Reggiano cheese
salt and freshly ground black pepper

Place the dried beans in a large saucepan or small pot. Roughly chop one stick of celery and one of the carrots and add along with 2 tablespoons of the olive oil, plus the garlic and the sage. Cover with water, bring to a boil and simmer until the beans are tender.

Meanwhile, hold the soft parts of the black cabbage leaves in one hand and the coarse central stem in the other, and pull the stem away. Wash the leaves carefully, then slice very thinly and set aside.

Finely slice the remaining celery stalk and carrot, and the onion. Heat about 6 tablespoons of the olive oil in a large pot, add the prepared vegetables and gently fry until soft. Add the cabbage and continue frying, stirring often, for another 5 minutes.

Bring a kettle of water to the boil. Pour about 1.4 litres (2½ pints) (6 cups) of the hot water onto the cabbage mixture and bring to a boil. Reduce the heat to a simmer and cook for 20–30 minutes.

When the beans are tender, drain and discard the flavouring vegetables. Pass half the beans through a vegetable mill to form a paste. Add the bean paste to the cabbage mixture and leave to simmer gently for another hour. Set the remaining beans aside.

Slice the courgettes into half-moon shapes. When the soup has cooked a further hour, add the courgettes and the remaining whole beans to the soup and simmer for another 10 minutes.

Cut the bread into cubes and place them at the bottom of a clean pot. Pour the soup over the top so that the bread starts to absorb the liquid. Set aside for 30 minutes or so.

The mixture will be very solid. Use a spoon to break up the bread and incorporate it with the other ingredients. Stir in a little water so that it's not too stiff, then reheat gently. When hot, add the cheese and remove from the heat immediately. Season with salt and pepper to taste, and serve drizzled with the remaining olive oil.

OPPOSITE: VALTER DEMONSTRATES THE ART OF ROLLING
FRESH PASTA.

RIGHT: ACTION AT THE STOVE.

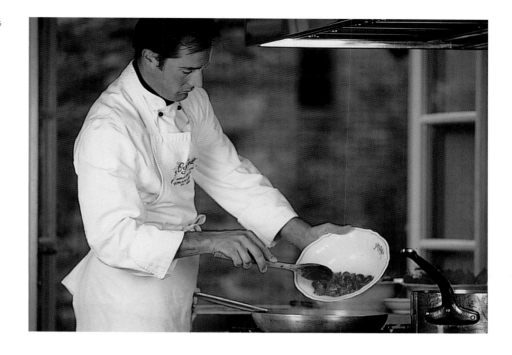

This filling is spooned along wide strips of fresh egg pasta dough that the class of five people has just prepared together, and rolled and lightly brushed with egg wash. Slightly longer strips, to compensate for the mounds of filling, are placed on top and gently pressed around the paste to enclose it. Then Valter brings out a small ravioli cutter — one of several kitchen tools his guests have enviously admired — and shows how to position it over the pasta and press down to form neat parcels.

The delicious ravioli are later cooked and tossed with a ready-made sauce of truffle-infused butter blended with mascarpone and served for lunch. Alongside are platters of tagliolini with cherry tomato and basil sauce, maltagliati or 'bad cuts' of pasta with a raw tomato sauce, and Valter's simple cheesecake with biscuit-crumb crust — demonstrated first in the cooking session in order to give the gelatine time to set.

The Coselli School of Tuscan Cuisine is a handy 25 minute drive from Pisa airport. The village of Coselli, sometimes called 'little Switzerland' thanks to its scenery, ambience and plentiful spring water, has only 100 inhabitants. The property can accommodate 24 guests, with a typical maximum of 16 in the kitchen for the cooking classes. These are run as scheduled programmes in spring and autumn, and on request through the rest of the year. A six-day itinerary typically incorporates eight hands-on classes, a trip to Pistoia market (the region's best),

visits to gourmet stores, artisan producers, restaurants and tours of nearby towns Lucca and Pisa. Non-cooking partners are more than welcome and can enjoy nearby sporting facilities such as tennis and golf, or simply laze around the serene estate's swimming pool, ornamental gardens, games room and library.

Although recently renovated, the estate is several centuries old. Count Cosimo Bernardini was a nobleman whose family owned several important properties and the estate at Coselli was his wild boar hunting lodge. Even today, the surrounding hills contain wild boar, and his descendants still reside in a villa close by. The count grew to love the place and gradually the estate became

THE ESTATE IS THE FORMER WILD BOAR HUNTING LODGE
OF COUNT COSIMO BERNARDINI, WHOSE DESCENDANTS
STILL LIVE IN THE AREA.

more prominent in his life. He planted formal Italian gardens, built a villa, chapel, stables, cellars, installed an olive press, ornamental ponds and masked fountains.

Chef and head teacher Valter Roman speaks excellent English thanks to years spent working in the United Kingdom. He met his British wife Julia while working as a pastry chef in Northumberland. He originally trained as a regular kitchen chef but found himself working on pastry as none of his colleagues ever wanted to do it. 'Most kitchen chefs hate pastry because they have no patience for measuring and being precise,' he says. 'Instinct is what they use to cook, and it's exactly what you don't need for pastry.' The result is that Valter has an unusual style of working, carefully measuring

some ingredients on digital scales, but confidently gauging by sight and adding handfuls of this and that on other occasions.

Valter's recipes are not written down precisely, partly because he wants to engage his students in the cooking process, to make them see and experience how it is done rather than simply following rules or instructions. His aim is to show people the 'true soul of the Italian kitchen'. Over dinner on the first evening, he suggests that the cuisine of the centre of the country is the most purely Italian, as food in the North is influenced by the French, and that of the South by the Spanish and North Africans. Many of the dishes are based on fresh produce: stuffed courgette (zucchini) flowers, potato gnocchi with basil pesto, fried artichokes with Pecorino cream,

THERE IS PLENTY OF TIME TO RELAX AND ENJOY THE
ROMANTIC ESTATE'S FACILITIES.

Amaretto peaches and fruit tarts. It's not all vegetarian however: day three features a trip into Chianti country, visiting the Antica Macelleria Falorni, which has been curing hams and other meats since 1700; day four a class in grilling Tuscany's esteemed Chianina steak; and day five a special fish supper featuring seafood risotto and pesce in cartoccio or fish cooked in a bag.

Having completed a sommelier's course, Valter takes pleasure in introducing guests informally to a variety of local wines during lunch and dinner. There is an organized tasting at the Verrazzano winery, which dates back to Etruscan times, and a further session with Raoul Ferrari, a local master of wine, who selects bottles to match each course for a dinner in the estate's wine library.

The programme also features a visit to a grappa producer, a fun lesson in making limoncello — Italy's sweet lemon liqueur, and a visit to Bei Nanni, one of Lucca's most famous coffee roasters.

The family-style kitchen, shared dining, friendly staff and simple yet luxuriously appointed rooms, make Borgo Bernardini an inviting compromise between a grand hotel and rustic farmhouse accommodation — what better way to delve into the soul of Tuscan cuisine?

Book courses at Borgo Bernadini via Gourmet on Tour (see right).

Other courses in Italy

Half-day to three-day courses including:
Noble Tuscan Cuisine — Learn about traditional Tuscan cuisine from a Michelin starred chef. Villa Il Patriarca offers half and full day lessons taught year round. No accommodation included.

Davina Cucina — Discover the art of eating and cooking in Florence. Enjoy hands-on cooking lessons or food lover's walking tours of the city. No accommodation included.

Three- to six-day courses including:
Three Perfect Days in Florence — This year-round course offers three days in Florence combining cooking lessons with vineyard visits. Accommodation included.

Villa San Michel — Based in Florence, discover the secrets of Italian cuisine in the kitchen alongside the experts. Accommodation included.

Contact: Gourmet on Tour
Berkeley Square House
2F Berkeley Square
Mayfair
London W1J 6BD
Tel UK +44 (0)20 7396 5550
Fax UK +44 (0)20 7900 1527
Tel US +1 800 504 9842
Fax US +1 800 886 2229
www.gourmetontour.com

Venice and Veneto Gourmet, Venice, Italy

Sara Cossiga set up Venice and Veneto Gourmet to combine her love of food and wine with her expertise in art and history. She offers a variety of intriguingly intellectual tours of Venice and the surrounding region, including sessions looking at the role of food in religious art, the impact of Turks on the local cuisine, water and well-heads around the city, and a very popular tour based on fish and fishermen in Venetian society. Visits to gourmet producers of rice, cheese and charcuterie are available, as are wine and food-matching sessions. The cookery classes are conducted in conjunction with three well-established Italian teachers, Maria Grazia Caló, and Roberta and Sebastiano Molani. Sara provides translation (and colourful historical detail) for English speakers.

Ever tried standing upright in a dinghy? On a wintry day in Venice, the canal a little choppy, the only thing preventing us toppling overboard was the fact that we were closely surrounded by several Venetians confidently balancing upright. Although not as comfortable as cruising the city's canals from a private gondola, forging the waters in this fashion was a sip of real Venetian life and, in its own way, rather romantic.

On Saturday morning, Sara Cossiga collected us from the ornate Palazzo Abadessa, where she had recommended we stay. Within minutes she had guided us through the warren of tiny streets to the bobbing boat. This was the quickest means of getting to the Rialto market, an important source of food for local residents and businesses. We surveyed the day's stalls, paying particular attention to the range of fish on offer, including gorgeous raw anchovies shining like sterling silver jewelery, large round clams with rose coloured-shells, tiny soles, mackerel, seabass and John Dory.

As Sara explained, in Venice fish was traditionally regarded as food for the poor, because there was so much of it, and fish dishes tended to be very plain. Only the wealthy had access to the prestige ingredients such as spices used for sauces, and the merchants tended to want to check the quality of what they were eating, so would favour fish cooked in little more than a bit of olive oil.

Then it was on to the cooking class. These take place in a stunning palazzo, one of the noble residences converted into blocks of apartments. Such buildings were originally intended to display the wealth of the merchants, and the sense of luxury lives on with a Murano glass chandelier, and colourful stencils decorating doorways, ceilings and beams with tones of yellow and green, red-brown and gold. The images of dolphins and shells are typical of the 18th century, and like many of these buildings, the rooms are tall enough for a mezzanine level. There is an intimate dining table in the kitchen, and a more formal table and seating in the main dining room.

VIEW OF THE GRAND CANAL IN VENICE.

ABOVE: FRESH SPAGHETTI, ITALY'S MOST FAMOUS EXPORT.

ABOVE RIGHT: LEARNING HOW TO MAKE FRESH PASTA.

Sara can't help tossing in some historical details: 'Decoration was one of the main aspects of Venetian arts. Colour means light. Venice was a marshy place with no hills, so colour enhanced the environment.'

Maria Grazia has chosen a typically Venetian winter menu and starts the lesson with an almond crocante, caramelizing sugar until it is dark toffee coloured in a pan on an elegant portable gas burner. She adds water, then stirs roasted, chopped almonds into the mixture. It's then poured quickly onto a sheet of silpat. Another sheet of silpat is placed on top, and Maria Grazia uses a rolling pin to flatten the mixture between the non-stick sheets. 'Crocante means

crispy,' says Sara. 'Roasting the almonds first brings out their flavour and also makes them crisp. If the nuts are too moist they will crystallize the sugar. It's tempting to lick the mixing spoon but don't — it's sizzling hot.'

The crocante mixture is taken up to the roof terrace to cool quickly. 'Crocante is now very popular,' says Sara. 'It used to be prepared as a sweet for children, once sugar became widely available, because it was easy for mothers to make and very nutritious.' Indeed, the ladies have a very Italian approach to the concept of healthy eating and reminisce about how they used to be served a non-alcoholic version of the classic rich dessert zabaglione

Venetian Mixed Seafood Risotto

9 large mussels

200 g (7 oz) prawns or shrimp

200 g (7 oz) squid

200 g (7 oz) white fish such as seabass
or monk fish

about 1–1.2 litres (1¾–2 pints) (4–5 cups)
fish stock

100 ml (3½ fl oz) (scant ½ cup) olive oil

1 garlic clove, crushed

a handful of fresh parsley, finely chopped

1 bay leaf

320 g (11 oz) (1½ cups) Vialone Nano rice
or risotto rice

a sprinkle of cognac

3 tablespoons butter

2 tablespoons freshly grated Parmesan cheese

salt and freshly ground black pepper

Maria Grazia uses a pointed wooden spoon with a hole in the centre for risotto, as it helps the mixture blend efficiently without crushing the ingredients. You can substitute other seafood varieties for those listed here. Simply add them in order according to their density.

Clean all the seafood as necessary. Place the mussels in a saucepan, cover and cook over a moderate heat for a few minutes, until they open. Remove from the heat and, when cool enough to handle, pick the meat from the shells and mince it finely. Set aside.

Peel the prawns or shrimp, and cut the squid and white fish into cubes, keeping them separate. Bring the fish stock to scalding point in a saucepan and keep hot. In a separate, wide saucepan, heat the olive oil. Add the garlic and a generous pinch of parsley and warm through. When aromatic, add the bay leaf and squid and gently fry for 2–3 minutes. Add the prawns or shrimp, white fish and minced mussels and cook, stirring, for another 1–2 minutes. Add the rice and stir until the grains become translucent.

Pour a ladle of stock over the rice mixture and stir until it is absorbed. Add another ladle of stock and cook, stirring, until it too has been absorbed. Repeat this process of adding stock and stirring for about 20 minutes in total, or until the rice is al dente – tender but with some bite.

Turn off the heat under the pan. Discard the bay leaf and sprinkle the risotto with the cognac. Dice the butter and stir it into the mixture together with the Parmesan and the rest of the parsley.

Season to taste, mix well and serve.

whenever they had the flu as children. 'It's considered very nutritious,' says Sara. 'So is grappa and milk — grappa latte. Served hot, it is good for coughs, colds and flu.'

Maria Grazia has already prepared a porridge of snow-white polenta and left it to cool on a slab. She heats a chargrill pan until it is smoking, cuts the polenta into large pieces and lays them on the grill. When the underside is striped black, she turns each piece with her fingers and cooks the other side. 'Cornmeal is typical of the Veneto and north of Italy,' says Sara. 'However it was not introduced until the 16th century. Prior to that, millet and chestnut flour were used. Today yellow cornmeal is very common but Venetians traditionally chose the white one.'

The grilled polenta bars are to be served with the local Sopressa Vincenza, a cured slicing sausage larger in diameter than most salumi, and which holds a DOP (designated origin of protection). 'It is supposed to be fatty and was historically eaten in winter in order to provide calories,' says Sara. 'To get rid of the fatty taste, which is a bit cloying, it is cooked briefly in a frying pan in two spoonfuls of wine and one spoonful of vinegar. The fat exudes in the heat and as soon as the liquid evaporates, it's ready. It's like braising. The dish should be salty and needs the polenta served alongside it for its neutrality.'

Also accompanying the Sopressa is a very simple salad of raw treviso, the bitter red

TRAVELLING BY GONDOLA IS THE MOST POPULAR WAY TO GET AROUND VENICE'S OFTEN NARROW CANALS.

leaves like elongated, sprawling radicchio, grown in nearby Treviso. 'There are some really stupid recipes using treviso,' says Sara candidly. 'They even make a sauce for cakes with it, but for me raw is best, or blanched in water and vinegar and then marinated in olive oil just to soften it — that's very good with raw meat.'

The main course is seafood risotto. 'Even we in Venice couldn't live without pasta any longer,' says Sara. 'It's the national dish, but rice is traditionally more important in this area. It has been grown in the Veneto region since the 15th century and little by little became more popular. There is a DOP on rice from Verona: Vialone Nano is short, round and ideal for risotto. It is a little bit smaller than arborio or carnaroli.' Of course, the ladies think it is a better risotto grain too.

Maria Grazia warms some olive oil in a saucepan and adds garlic and parsley — no onion. Surely risotto always begins with frying an onion? But no. 'The broth is flavoured with onion already,' Sara explains. 'When risotto is made with fish, the fish is sweet, so there is no need for the sweetness of onion. We would only use onion in a risotto that had more spicy or salty ingredients.'

Indeed, the unifying theme of the dishes we are shown, and of Venetian cooking, is the careful balance of sweet and sour flavours. 'We don't use sweet and hot, or sweet and spicy combinations,' says Sara. 'For us it has to be sweet and sour.'

Courses currently available

Wine tastings

Sample three different local wines and learn about their history, and organic characteristics as well as how to match them with local foods.

Three hour tours, including:

Depictions of Food in Venetian Art — The perfect mix of food and art; explore the history of Venetian society with a guided tour through the districts of San Polo and Castello. *Venice & the Turks* — A historical tour of Venice stopping to view paintings and the visual arts of the Renaissance.

Contact: Sara Cossiga
www.venicevenetogourmet.com
Venezia, Italia
Tel/fax +39 041 2750 687

Kimberley Lodge, Russell, New Zealand

Modern New Zealand cuisine is often linked to Pacific Rim and fusion styles of cooking. It takes abundant fresh produce — seafood, meat, fruit and vegetables — and puts them together in creative combinations influenced by a wide variety of cultures, including Polynesia, Asia, Europe and the Middle East. But it's not just the ingredients and the way they're cooked that is interesting — the easy-going manner in which they are served is special too. There is plenty of opportunity for outdoor eating, whether that be lunch on a sunny terrace with stunning views or a feast down at the beach, and restaurants and cafés offer plenty of platters to share, making meals relaxed and convivial. Simply prepared fresh seafoods, such as oysters, crayfish and the internationally renowned green-lipped mussels, are another distinguishing feature and these match perfectly with the Sauvignon Blanc for which the country has also developed an outstanding worldwide reputation. A few days at Kimberley Lodge offers a taste of it all.

Russell may seem like a quaint small town today, but it was New Zealand's first capital. Known as Kororareka in the early 19th century, it lies on the northern arm of the northern isle and boasts two of New Zealand's oldest buildings, the Duke of Marlborough Hotel and the Anglican Christ Church, the country's first Christian meeting house. The town was not always dignified. As a whaling and sealing area once known as the hellhole of the Pacific, the businesses that first sprung up in this district were brothels that attracted and

serviced sea farers, escaped convicts and other rough trade. The neat whiteboard properties that line the bay are more civilized than days of yore, making the idea of staying the night just as attractive — but for very different reasons.

Captain Cook named the dazzling body of waters that Russell overlooks the Bay of Islands (there are 144 of them) in 1769. Kimberley Lodge, which sits on a bluff overlooking the bay, is just a few minutes' walk from Russell's Wharf. From there it is

OPPOSITE: A HANDFUL OF FRESH OYSTERS.

RIGHT: KIMBERLEY LODGE.

Green-lipped Mussel and Saffron Shooter

Typical of the contemporary style of New Zealand cuisine, this classy shooter-style soup by Virginia Holloway is ideal for a cocktail party and best accompanied by chilled Sauvignon Blanc. Green-lipped mussels are native to New Zealand but are marketed worldwide and should be relatively easy to buy.

MAKES 20

20 green-lipped mussels
½ teaspoon saffron threads
1 tablespoon olive oil
1 onion, finely chopped
2 garlic cloves, finely sliced
½ stick celery, finely chopped
2 sprigs of lemon thyme
½ teaspoon black peppercorns
3 parsley stalks
250 ml (8 fl oz) (1 cup) Sauvignon Blanc
   wine
2 tablespons butter, softened, plus
   3 tablespoons butter, chilled and diced
4 tablespoons cream
freshly ground white pepper
a small handful of chives, snipped,
   to garnish

Thoroughly scrub and debeard the mussels and set them aside.

Put a little water on to boil in a kettle. Meanwhile, in a dry frying pan, toast the saffron threads briefly until fragrant, stirring constantly to prevent burning. Transfer the saffron to a mortar and crush it, then add 50ml (2 fl oz) (¼ cup) boiling water from the kettle and leave to steep.

Heat the olive oil in a small lidded pot. Add half the chopped onion, plus the garlic, celery, thyme, peppercorns and parsley stalks and sauté them until the onion has softened.

Add the mussels and wine and cover with the lid of the pot. As the mussels start opening, remove them to a tray and keep them covered with damp cloth to prevent drying out. Strain the liquor from the pot through a fine sieve and reserve it, but discard the solids.

In medium saucepan, melt the 2 tablespoons of softened butter. Add the remaining onion, cover and cook over a low heat so that the onion sweats without colouring. Pour in the saffron water and continue cooking until the onion is soft. Add the reserved mussel cooking liquor and bring the mixture to a boil. Then add the cream, return to the boil, reduce the heat to a gentle simmer and cook for 5 minutes. Season with white pepper.

Remove the mussels from the shells. If they are cool, warm them quickly in a little of the broth. Place a mussel in each shooter glass.

Using a stick blender, add the chilled, diced butter to the broth and blend until thick and foamy. Pour the broth over the mussels in the shooter glasses and garnish with the chives. Serve immediately.

possible to arrange day cruises, jet boats, whale- and dolphin-watching expeditions, diving, sailing and fishing charters. The region is famous for game fishing and sailing. Golfers have much to enjoy here as well. But as Virginia and Craig Holloway of Kimberley Lodge aim to prove, Russell is also a fine destination for food lovers.

Typical of New Zealand's prestigious lodge accommodation — a type of luxury B&B or very small boutique-style country hotel — Kimberley Lodge is housed in a mansion built in 1989 from local timber in colonial style. The tranquil rooms have high ceilings, crystal chandeliers and balconies offering spectacular views. There is a lush sub-tropical garden and swimming pool on the property.

Virginia is the well-travelled chef at the lodge and has worked in France, Scotland and Australia. She favours organic fruit and vegetables, fresh local and regional produce, and exciting ingredient combinations served with elegance and panache. The table d'hôte dining room at the lodge features ingredients such as Orongo oysters, green-lipped mussels, New Zealand lamb, as well as a cellar of New Zealand wines. A typical menu by Virginia could include dishes such as tom yum soup with seared king prawn; mussel dumplings with pear and rocket salad and a light curried sauce; salmon confit in a spiced saffron broth with soba noodle fritter; and chocolate cake with beetroot ice cream and candied almonds. She happily caters to guests' specific tastes and dietary requirements, and will

prepare the catch of any guests who have been fishing — it can even be smoked to take on a gourmet picnic or preserve it for the journey home.

When it came to devising her cookery classes, Virginia went for a unique style that seems to suit the area and nature of the property well. You don't have to attend a set schedule of proposed dates. There is a suggested two or three days of activity, but she will also work around the interests of the individual guests. As with her cuisine, much of the focus is on local produce, and who wouldn't make use of all that magnificent water?

Day one may involve a trip to the ocean, gathering mussels from the rocks, and collecting kina, the New Zealand sea egg,

a traditional Maori food found at low tide in rock crevices and under ledges. Fishing and collecting 'kai-moana' or food of the sea remains a popular pastime in New Zealand. The ocean visit may also yield crayfish and fresh flounder, a deep-water flat fish popular in the southern hemisphere and reminiscent of Dover sole.

Then it's a drive to one of the local oyster farms to harvest and shuck fresh oysters, before a tour of a local olive grove, where there is a tasting session and lunch. New Zealanders have readily adopted and adapted Mediterranean cuisine and now have also taken the olive tree to heart. Just as the country proved suitable for grape growing, now it turns out that several regions have the

potential to produce good olives and olive oils, and the European Commission is watching with concern. The fear, for the northern hemisphere at least, is that New World countries such as New Zealand, Australia and the U.S. will prove as savvy at developing their table olive and oil industries as they were at taking on the traditional European winemakers.

It's into Virginia's professional kitchen for the second day of the Kimberley Lodge course. This exciting and inspiring session involves working with her to prepare the foods collected, and cook a full formal dinner for service in the dining room that evening. It's an opportunity to get to grips with a dynamic, innovative culinary style under her watchful, kindly guidance.

The optional day three includes a visit to two local wineries. Omata was the site of the first European settlement in New Zealand, the location of the first provincial store, and in 1837 the scene of the country's first aggravated burglary (for which the culprits were sent to Sydney for trial and hanging). Omata Estate Winery produces bold, full-bodied wines with rich flavours, in particular varieties such as Chardonnay, Shiraz (Syrah) and Merlot.

Marsden Estate on the citrus-covered slopes of nearby Kerikeri is named after Samuel Marsden, who introduced the grapevine to New Zealand with 100 plantings at Kerikeri in 1819. Today Marsden Estate grows Pinot Gris,

OPPOSITE: HOUSES ON THE WATERFRONT IN RUSSELL.

RIGHT: THE BALCONY VIEW LOOKING OUT TO SEA FROM
KIMBERLEY LODGE.

Chardonnay, Merlot, Malbec, Pinotage, Cabernet Sauvignon and Chambourcin. Before heading back to the lodge there is a stop at a boutique chocolatier in Kerikeri that makes products by hand using first-rate raw materials. Rich macadamia nuts are a favourite ingredient, turned here into a variety of sweet treats including shortbread and brittle. Guests watch the confectionery being made and taste various samples.

Kimberley Lodge is situated approximately three-hours' drive north from Auckland and 30 minutes drive south from Kerikeri Airport. The Bay of Islands alone is worth the journey, but what a delight to be able to delve into the secrets of contemporary New Zealand food and wine as well.

Also in New Zealand

Top caterer Ruth Pretty is a doyenne of New Zealand cookery and runs a top-class school in the tranquil region of Te Horo on the Kapiti Coast. Guest presenters and food personalities supplement her own classes, which finish with a leisurely lunch on the verandah. Accommodation is available at a luxury lodge in the vicinity of the school. Visit www.ruthpretty.co.nz for further details.

Courses currently available

This two- to three-day course is currently the only course on offer by Kimberley Lodge. Includes gathering shellfish from the sea, visits to an oyster farm and a vineyard, and hands-on cookery lessons where you will learn to prepare and cook the foods collected.

Contact: Kimberley Lodge
PO Box 166
Pitt Street
Russell
Bay of Islands
Tel: +64 9 403 7090
Fax: +64 9 403 7239
www.lodges.co.nz

Nick Nairn Cook School,
Trossachs, Scotland

Scotland is renowned in continental Europe, and especially France, for its excellent produce. Think of the country's superb smoked salmon, grass-fed Aberdeen Angus beef and full-flavoured raspberries. But, having suffered from the post-war encouragement of intensive factory farming, and a perspective that food is fuel rather than something to be enjoyed, the Scots themselves have only really begun to appreciate their outstanding natural food resources in the last 20 years or so. At the forefront of this exciting period of reassessment is tv-chef Nick Nairn, who through programmes such as *Wild Harvest, Island Harvest,* and *Ready, Steady, Cook,* has promoted the best of Scottish cuisine around the world. Now, at his cookery school in the scenic Trossachs region, he works with an expert team of chefs to show people in 'real life' how to make the most of fine ingredients.

Nick Nairn bends down over the stovetop set in the demonstration area of his cookery school and, with one hand cupped behind his right ear, looks comically up at the engrossed audience. 'What's that?' he asks them as the pot sizzles noisily. 'A happy pan!' He straightens his back and looks serious for a moment. 'Listen for the sizzle. A sizzle is a happy pan doing its job. Sizzle equals water. The juices are coming out and the meat is caramelizing. Now listen...'

Bending down again, hand behind the ear, eyebrows raised quizzically, he pauses so the class can hear the sounds emanating from the pot. 'The sizzle is slowing down.' His voice slows down in tandem. 'The juices have evaporated away, so there's less to boil. If there's no noise, it's a *sad pan*, there's not enough heat.' Picking up the pace again, Nick moves his arms around expressively. 'If there's flames and burning, it's an *angry pan*.' He stops, bashful, knowing he looks a bit silly. 'The reason I'm talking to you like this is because I want you to remember.'

When Nick Nairn first opened his school in the romantic rural setting of Scotland's Port of Menteith, he was already a BBC television chef known around the world.

He envisioned days would be spent teaching gourmets the intricacies of butter sauces, but has subsequently realized most people need to learn culinary basics such as how to fry.

Nevertheless, in the case of his New Scottish Cookery classes, explanation of the basics is cleverly woven into a balanced dinner party menu achieveable for home cooks. 'There are probably six people in the world who can pull off the modern trend for molecular gastronomy, so let's leave it to them. Most people don't often get to taste good produce properly cooked and left to speak for itself.

'I've been cooking professionally for 20 years,' he continues, 'and in that time I've reduced my philosophy to three things you must have to serve good food: produce, technique and harmony. Produce, meaning good quality ingredients, is king. Technique? Well, it's no good buying a wonderful turbot then leaving it in the fridge for three days, then boiling it for half an hour. And harmony: the flavours have to all come together. To help achieve this, remember there are certain combinations that just work really well together, such as tomatoes and basil, lamb and rosemary, or steak and chips.'

SCOTLAND'S HISTORIC TROSSACHS REGION IS KNOWN FOR ITS SCENIC BEAUTY AND OUTDOOR PURSUITS.

NICK NAIRN (LEFT) AT THE STOVE WITH THE COOKERY
SCHOOL'S HEAD TEACHER, JOHN WEBBER.

Early in the session he emphasises the importance of planning simple menus and making as much as possible in advance. Yet even those people who are used to this idea, and regularly choose no-cook starters and chilled desserts, don't seem to realize how very much can be prepared ahead of time. Using the day's main course of pigeon breasts with game sauce, mashed potatoes, and a cabbage and bacon sauté to illustrate, Nick lists the advantages: 'The mash can be made three days in advance. The gravy can be made one month in advance. The vegetable garnish can be made in advance and reheated in the microwave. So when it comes to the night of the dinner party, you only have to cook the pigeon breasts. These take three minutes, and in fact they too can be cooked in advance and reheated.'

Without question, he says, the last-minute management of pans on the stovetop come serving time is one of the things amateur chefs find hardest. 'It takes experience and practice,' he admits. 'Television programmes and cookery books have raised people's expectations.'

But it's Nick's clear perception of what can and cannot be expected of home cooks that makes his classes so empowering. 'Cooking is easy. Brain surgery is quite hard. Molecular biology is difficult,' he says, only half-joking. The fact that, as a chef, he is self-taught, no doubt informs his opinion. 'Cooking is *not* a particularly hard thing to do.

Lasagne of Smoked Haddock and Peas

SERVES 2

FOR THE NAGE BUTTER SAUCE:

300 ml (½ pint) (1¼ cups) good-quality
　fresh vegetable stock
100 g (3½ oz) (1 stick) cold butter, diced
½ teaspoon lemon juice
freshly ground black pepper

4 sheets of lasagne
2 fillets smoked haddock, about
　175 g (6 oz) each, skinned
100 g (3½ oz) (1 scant cup) frozen peas
2 tablespoons chopped chives
a few drops of lemon juice
sea salt flakes, such as Maldon
freshly ground white pepper

A good example of Nick Nairn's 'New Scottish Cookery', this wintry recipe uses one of Scotland's most famous traditional ingredients, smoked haddock, in a thoroughly modern manner. These days smoked haddock is produced in many countries, including the U.S. However, like many popular foods, there are well-made brands, and others less so. 'Try and avoid radioactive-looking, orange smoked haddock,' says Nick. 'It seems to glow in the dark, so heaven knows what it tastes like.' For ease of serving and presentation, he suggests finishing each portion in separate small saucepans.

To make the nage butter sauce, pour the vegetable stock into a small saucepan. Place over a high heat and bring to a boil. Boil hard to reduce until it is dark, thick and sticky, and the volume of liquid in the pan equals about 4 tablespoons.

Reduce the heat under the pan to low and add the butter. Use a hand-blender to blend the contents of the pan until the butter melts and the sauce becomes light and frothy in texture.

Add the lemon juice and pepper, adjusting the seasoning to taste. Set the sauce aside in a warm place while you prepare the rest of the dish.

In a large pot of boiling salted water, cook the lasagne sheets until they are 'al dente' or tender but retaining some bite. Drain and set aside.

Divide the nage butter sauce between two small saucepans and warm it until just under boiling point. Add the fish to each pan and simmer very gently for 3–4 minutes or until the fish is almost tender, turning the fish over about halfway through cooking to coat with the sauce.

Divide the peas and the pasta between the two pans and warm through for 2–3 minutes. Meanwhile, warm two shallow serving bowls. Add most of the chopped chives plus a few drops of lemon juice to the saucepans. Taste and add salt and pepper as desired, plus a bit more lemon juice if required. Allow the dish to heat through for a minute longer.

Arrange the pasta, fish and sauce nicely in the warmed bowls. Scatter with the remaining chives and serve immediately.

LEFT: NICK'S VERSION OF CRANACHAN, A CLASSIC
SCOTTISH DESSERT OF TOASTED PINHEAD OATMEAL,
RASPBERRIES, WHISKY AND CREAM.

OPPOSITE LEFT: SCOTTISH LAMB IS EXCELLENT. NICK
RECOMMENDS THE NATIVE ORGANIC BLACK-FACED
BREEDS AND SHETLAND LAMB.

OPPOSITE RIGHT: NICK IN THE SCHOOL'S HERB AND
VEGETABLE GARDEN.

Professional chefs have simply done
every single task five thousand, ten
thousand, fifteen thousand times, so they
get very quick at doing things, and very
instinctive. That's the difference between
professional and amateur.'

The point is best illustrated when the
class turns to vegetable preparation.
No one can chop and slice as fast as the
pros all seem to. 'It takes a chef a year to
learn how to use a knife properly,' says
Nick. 'It's a long, hard apprenticeship. If
you are going to learn to do it, you must
use the same knife for every job. If you
only use a chef's knife three times a
week, you'll never get the hang of it. The
action is half slicing and half chopping.
All the movement is in the wrist. For the
first while it will feel awful. The trick is
to get it precise first and then go faster.'

Nick is not wearing chef whites; he's wearing jeans and underneath his apron is a 'South Park' t-shirt. When he curses, everybody laughs. The informal approach enhances rather than detracts from the teaching, and certainly does not compromise the professionalism. As Nick is very careful to state, every chef teaching and assisting at the school has worked in Michelin-starred restaurants. The head teacher, John Webber, achieved his first star many years ago as head chef at the world-renowned Gidleigh Park Hotel in Devon. In addition, the annual programme features guest appearances by some of Britain's top food experts.

After preparing their three-course lunch and enjoying plentiful wine and coffee, the friendly participants, many of whom have received the day's course as a Christmas gift, return to the demonstration area to watch Nick produce three more contemporary supper dishes. Two of the group are allergic to gluten, but their requirements are handled with grace. 'We've found one in 20 of our students are on gluten-free diets,' Nick reveals. He goes on to explain his own interest in reducing the amount of salt in food, especially bread. 'People say you need salt for flavour but that's rubbish. It's because they don't use good flour.'

Having sold his eponymous restaurant in Glasgow, Nick is reluctant to go back into that part of the industry and is for the time being devoting all his attention to the cookery school and its expansion. With characteristic determination he concludes: 'I won't be happy until it is the best cookery school in the world.'

Courses currently available

Recreational classes including:
Informal Dinner Party (Spring, Summer, Autumn, Winter) — Flexible dishes that emphasise the fun and pleasure of cooking at home for guests. Dishes chosen for the day are designed to be served according to the style of the dinner party. Attention is given to pre-preparation and planning. The menus for this day change seasonally.

One-day or one-week masterclasses including:
Meat, Poultry and Game — Preparing chicken for sauté and grilling, Roman chicken, confit of duck, pot roast rabbit, best end of lamb with provincial vegetables, black pudding with apples. *Desserts and Puddings* — Crème fraîche mousse, apple crisps, puff pastry, sable pastry, blind-baked pastry shells and puff pastry apple tarts.

Guest chef classes — An exciting opportunity to cook with some of the industry's biggest names including Nick Nairn, Maxine Clark, Phil Vickery and Paul Rankin.

Contact: Nick Nairn Cook School
Port of Menteith
Stirling
Scotland FK8 3JZ
Tel +44 (0)1877 385603
Fax +44 (0)1877 385 643
www.nairnscookschool.com

Raffles Culinary Academy
Singapore, Singapore

You don't have to be staying at Raffles Hotel to enjoy a morning's demonstration and lunch at the hotel's genteel Culinary Academy. It's a fun way to experience an elegant slice of Singaporean life, and an interesting contrast to the bustle of the hawker centre, the fast food stalls and Orchard Road shopping trips — and no less authentic. The range of classes on offer encompasses the expertise of the hotel's brigade of chefs, some demonstrating traditional Chinese, Indian and Malaysian dishes, others teaching haute cuisine and patisserie techniques from Europe, or the latest fusion ideas. You won't have room for tiffin after sampling all the dishes in class, but a wander around the prestige shops and a leisurely afternoon cocktail in the famous Long Bar should round the day off nicely.

Raffles Hotel first opened in 1887 as the Beach House, a bungalow that looked very different from the grand white building it is today. It was founded by four Armenian brothers: Martin, Tigran, Aviet and Arshak Sarkies, and over the years became famous as a haunt for writers, royalty and other celebrities. 'Feed at Raffles when visiting Singapore,' said author Rudyard Kipling, and people have followed that reliable advice ever since.

Herein lies the problem. Raffles Hotel was declared a National Monument in Singapore in 1987, and today most of its visitors come as tourists rather than resident travellers. The exquisite colonial architecture (the property was reopened in 1991 after extensive restoration), and leafy courtyards make it a wonderfully serene place to wander. That is, as long as you can avoid the weekend busloads of tourists. The group identification stickers on their chests make them easy to spot as they are shepherded by guides quickly round the property and into the Tiffin Room for their buffet tea, or the Long Bar for a Singapore Sling, the world-famous cocktail invented at the hotel.

The Raffles Culinary Academy lies in a more sedate part of the building, the elegant concourse shopping centre near the open-air Doc Cheng's restaurant. It was launched in 1995 with the objectives of showcasing Singapore's culinary community, and giving the hotel's patrons an opportunity to learn the secrets of Raffles dishes and access the expertise of resident and visiting chefs. The list of instructors is as multicultural as the cuisine of the hotel's various dining rooms, and they lead half-day demonstration classes in subjects as diverse as Indian Breads, Healthy Tofu Recipes, Noodle Appetizers, Plantation Fusion, Kuih-Kuih Making, French Sauces and Stocks, Confiserie Techniques, English Specialities and Hot and Cold Tapas. English translation and commentary is provided, and the schedule is designed so that it is quite possible to attend a month of classes without ever returning to the same dishes.

Sixty per cent of the academy's clients are repeat customers. There is invariably a contingent of Singapore's Tai-tai (society women), tourists, and Westerners who

THE MAGNIFICENT EXTERIOR OF THE RAFFLES HOTEL.

Pandan Chiffon Cake

Pastry and dessert classes are extremely popular at Raffles Culinary Academy, and this recipe by chef Bernard Decaix shows how typical Asian flavours such as coconut milk and pandan (also known as screwpine) can be combined in a delicate cake.

SERVES 8

300 ml (½ pint) (1 ⅓ cups) coconut milk
150 g (5 oz) (heaped ¾ cup) caster
   sugar, plus 1 tablespoon extra
9 pandan leaves (found at Oriental grocers)
100ml (3½ fl oz) (scant ½ cup) warm water
9 eggs
150 g (5 oz) (1 cup) cake flour
½ teaspoon baking powder
¼ teaspoon salt
½ teaspoon pandan essence
½ teaspoon cream of tartar

Preheat the oven to 160°C (325°F) Gas Mark 3. Pour the coconut milk into a saucepan and add the 150 g (5 oz) caster sugar. Bring to a boil, stirring to disolve the sugar. Set aside to cool.

Meanwhile, make some pandan juice. Cut the pandan leaves into small pieces and place in a small food processor or blender bowl. Add the warm water and process to give a thin purée. Strain this purée through a fine muslin cloth to give the pandan juice (you will not need all of it) and set aside.

Separate the eggs, placing the 9 egg whites in one large clean mixing bowl, and 8 egg yolks in another. Discard the extra egg yolk, or save for use on another occasion.

Sift the cake flour, baking powder and salt into a large mixing bowl.

When the coconut mixture has cooled, pour it onto the egg yolks, whisking well, then whisk in 2 tablespoons of the pandan juice you have made, and the pandan essence.

Add the sifted flour mixture to the coconut mixture and stir until the batter is smooth. Set aside.

Whisk the egg whites lightly. Add the cream of tartar and the extra 1 tablespoon caster sugar through a sieve and continue whisking until the mixture is stiff and white. Be careful not to over-beat the whites or they will become too dry.

Gently fold half the beaten egg whites into the batter and mix well. Fold in the remaining egg whites, working very lightly with a spatula but ensuring the mixture is thoroughly combined.

Pour the batter into an ungreased chiffon cake mould (extra deep ring mould) 24 cm (9½ inches) in diameter and 10 cm (4 inches) deep. Level the surface and bake for about 45 minutes or until golden brown.

Remove the cake from the oven and invert the mould on a wire rack but do not try to lift off the mould. Leave to cool for 1 hour. When the cake has cooled, use a long, fine palate knife to loosen the sides of the cake from the tin and turn it out.

have made their home (at least temporarily) in Singapore and want to learn as much as possible about the local cuisine during their stay. 'This is the best lunch in Singapore,' said one as he tucked into an intricate dish of prawns and broccoli balancing on a mushroom base, one of the recipes demonstrated during a class on auspicious foods for Chinese New Year.

Some may find the atmosphere at the academy too rarefied, and not reflective of the vibrant 'street food' scene for which Singapore has become so renowned. Even a class featuring popular hawker centre dishes such as Hainanese Chicken Rice will teach how to make them the Raffles way. But grand old Raffles is characteristic of Singapore in its own right, and its spin on street food dishes is in itself interesting.

Professionals who already have some knowledge of Oriental and Asian cuisines may find the introductory nature of the classes a little frustrating. Those who are new to the subject, and amateur cooks, will enjoy the demonstrations for the leisure activity that they are designed to be, and perhaps relax that there is no requirement for them to produce the chefs' sometimes quite challenging dishes in public. Certainly it's good to see how a professional uses unfamiliar ingredients, and experience how they should taste, before purchasing them yourself. In addition, Raffles offers classes in topics such as how to plan a party, home dining, wines and etiquette, as well as tailor-made programmes for groups of up to 20.

TRADITIONAL STEAMERS USED TO COOK AND SERVE FOOD.

THE RENOWNED SINGAPORE SLING COCKTAIL.

The class in traditional dim sum dishes of Chinese New Year revealed more than just recipes and cooking techniques. Cultural traditions — some may say superstitions — informed the whole menu. Indeed, the entire point is that the dishes are rich in symbolism and meaning, as the Chinese believe that what you eat in the New Year will improve your good fortune for the year to come.

Deliciously nutty and crumbly sesame seed pastries were flavoured with red bean paste and deep-fried to a golden colour that represents gold and therefore prosperity. Chicken was served, for it symbolizes prosperity too. Noodle dishes were made using full-length noodles, as the strands symbolize long life, and the Chinese believe the longer, the better.

RIGHT: SINGAPORE SATAY.

FAR RIGHT: CHOPSTICKS ARE THE TRADITIONAL DINING
TOOLS IN SINGAPORE.

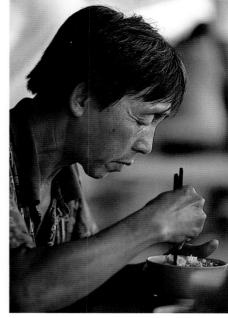

Guests sit in a refined atmosphere, watching the demonstration at the stylish central counter, taking notes in the dark green folder of recipes provided. After a question and answer session, they move to the group of round, linen-swathed dining tables at the back of the room for lunch, ready to sample the procession of dishes just cooked. The mood switches from formal to jovial as tea is served, experiences shared and the food enjoyed and discussed — however the ambience of dignity and reserve never quite dissipates. This is Raffles, after all.

Also in Singapore

At-Sunrice offers early morning guided strolls through its spice garden, after which visitors go back to the school's kitchen to make spice pastes.

It also offers a range of leisure classes in cuisines including Nonya, Malay, Chinese, Indian and New Asian. See www.at-sunrice.com for details. Davagi Sanmugum is one of Singapore's leading food authorities and in her home cooking studio offers hands-on and demonstration classes covering various aspects of speciality Asian cuisines including Indian and Indonesian. She also leads children's cooking workshops. Visit www.epicureanworld.com.sg.

A short drive from the city centre, and not far from the airport, friendly teacher Ruqxana runs 'up close and personal' home-style classes. For further details visit www.cookerymagic.com.

Courses currently available

One-day courses including:

Soups and Spices — Learn how to use a range of different aromatic ingredients to make soups and other dishes.

Seafood Casserole Cooking — In this course, experience cooking with fish and shellfish to make wonderful casseroles.

Desserts with Fresh Fruit — A course on how to make professional looking and tasting desserts all with fresh fruit. No accommodation included.

Contact: Raffles Culinary Academy
Raffles Hotel
1 Beach Road
Singapore 189673
Tel: + 65 6412 1256
Fax: +65 6339 7013
www.raffleshotel.com/culinaryacademy.html

Culinary Adventures, Barcelona, Spain

Culinary Adventures was set up by Marta Angula and Anne Marie Aznarez to provide scheduled and tailor-made gourmet food and wine tours throughout Spain. These may be as brief as a morning cookery class followed by lunch, or a week-long journey through a particular region, taking in restaurants, tapas bars, tastings, seminars and visits to artisan food producers. In Catalonia, currently seen as one of the world's culinary hotspots thanks to innovative chef Ferran Adria, one-day tours can be constructed to take in modernist art as well as food, or a leisurely journey into the north of the area, exploring seaside towns and tasting Spanish wines. Cooking classes for a minimum of two people are available in Madrid, Seville, San Sebastián on the Costa Brava, as well as in vibrant Barcelona.

The long-haired, short-bearded young fishmonger takes a large, severe, half-moon-shaped knife blade and begins to dissect a cuttlefish. He looks as though he belongs in a grunge rock band, but his vocation is actually to be the best fish supplier in Barcelona.

'Most suppliers get their fish from the central market near the airport, where fish comes from all over the world, including Africa and Argentina,' says our guide, chef Jaume Brichs. 'This one buys from suppliers at the port in Barcelona each afternoon. It's fresh, local and the most expensive.'

As Jaume is careful to explain, shopping for seafood in Barcelona's La Boqueria (no one uses its correct name of Saint Joseph's market) is not a simple matter of expensive equals good, cheap equals bad. 'See that girl over there? She runs a cheaper stall because it is in a cheap rent area of the market. She sells really fresh fish, but they are the less expensive varieties. That mackerel, for example, is very good and very fresh as well as very cheap.'

A few steps away however is a fish stall on which he does not look favourably. 'The hake is 6 euros,' says Jaume. 'That means it's not from the Mediterranean. Hake from the Med would be 18 or 21 euros. So as you can see there are some people here who shop on price rather than taste, and this market caters to all people. We know that when a product is top price it is also top quality, because there are so many stalls and suppliers that La Boqueria is highly competitive.'

He was keen to find cuttlefish just a few inches long, in the hope that he could show us a dish of baby cuttlefish and white beans, but no luck today. Instead he is excited to see gulas, a sticky white mass of the tiniest baby elvers, sold at a premium due to their quality and rarity.

Behind Jaume's kind, dark eyes, his brain is constantly flicking through his mental recipe index cards, deciding what he could make with each ingredient, and what else would be needed to complete each dish. 'We can buy anything you want,' he says. 'What do you like?'

THE COOKING OF CATALONIA, LIKE ITS ARCHITECTURE,

IS TODAY RENOWNED FOR INNOVATION.

GAZPACHO, REFRESHING IN THE MEDITERRANEAN HEAT.

He points to a pile of what looks like grey-white velour fabric scattered with salt crystals. 'These are really, really good,' he says, holding up his thumb and first finger in a circle to emphasise the point. 'Cod fish tripes.'

Cod, especially bacalao or salt cod, seems to be found at every turn in this market, and features on every Catalan menu. At his favourite bacalao stall, Jaume and the friendly white-aproned lady behind the counter attempt to explain the intricate differences between the myriad types on display, providing samples to taste as they go. Esqueixada, we learn, is not just the name of Catalonia's famous salt cod salad. The word means 'to shred', and the salt cod used in the salad should always be shredded by hand, not with a knife.

After coffee and a custard-filled pastry, we pile into the car and head from Las Ramblas, the street on which La Boqueria is based, to the Parc du Guell area of the city. Our cooking class takes place in the small kitchen of an elegant townhouse, though when there are more participants the sessions are held in a professional teaching kitchen.

Jaume puts out various plates of food for us to sample, some picked up at the market, others bought earlier. There are four types of olives — 'dead' ones from Aragon that are black and dry, big fleshy Caspe olives, tiny bitter Arbequinas, and 'gazpacho' or prepared olives in a chunky

Cuttlefish Fideua

Although some restaurants in Spain serve this hearty dish as a starter, it's really a main course or meal in itself. Lowering the quantity of cuttlefish would make it lighter. If you can't find fideua noodles, break vermicelli or other thin wheat noodles into short pieces about 2.5 cm (1 inch) long and use them instead.

SERVES 4

2 tomatoes

a pinch of saffron threads

1 cuttlefish, about 800 g (1 lb 12 oz)

4–5 tablespoons extra virgin olive oil

2 mild onions, chopped

1 red bell pepper, deseeded and chopped

1 garlic clove

salt

2–3 handfuls of chopped parsley

2 litres (3½ pints) (9 cups) fish stock

500 g (1 lb) (4 cups) fideua pasta, or other thin, short dried noodles

Put a kettle of water on to boil. Place the tomatoes in a large heat-proof jug or mixing bowl, scoring a cross in the base with a knife if desired, and pour some boiling water from the kettle over them. Allow to stand for about 1 minute to scald, then drain the water away.

Peel the skins off the tomatoes and cut in half horizontally. Scoop out the seeds using a teaspoon or small knife and discard them. Chop the tomato flesh roughly and set aside.

Place the saffron in a dry pan over a moderate heat and toast, stirring constantly, until fragrant and crisp, but not browned. Transfer the saffron to a little heat-proof bowl and add a few tablespoons of hot water from the kettle. Set aside to infuse.

Cut the cuttlefish into bit-sized cubes. Heat 2–3 tablespoons of olive oil in a wide frying pan or skillet. Gently fry the cuttlefish until tinged golden, stirring occasionally, then remove from the pan and set aside on a plate.

In the same oil, slowly sweat the chopped onion over a low heat so that it cooks without browning. When the liquid in the pan has completely evaporated, add the red bell pepper and continue cooking until it has softened, then add the tomato and continue frying until the mixture has

the consistency of jam — thick and fairly sticky.

Meanwhile, pound the garlic with some salt in a mortar until fine, then work in the chopped parsley until it is well combined but still fresh and vibrant — do not attempt to make it a paste. Stir in the saffron water. Set aside.

Add the cooked cuttlefish to the vegetable mixture, then remove the pan from the heat and set aside.

In a saucepan, heat the fish stock until it is hot but not boiling. Meanwhile, in a paella pan, or a wide and flat-bottomed skillet or low-sided pot, heat another 2 tablespoons of olive oil. Add the pasta pieces and fry over a medium heat, stirring often, until they are lightly toasted (some will turn brown).

Add the cuttlefish and vegetable mixture to the pan of fried pasta, then pour in the hot fish stock. Add some seasoning and mix gently but thoroughly. Bring the mixture to a simmer and cook for about 2 minutes.

Pour the saffron and parsley mixture into the fideua, stir briefly and continue cooking for another 2 minutes. Then remove the pan from the heat and allow the dish to rest for a few more minutes before serving.

vinegary marinade studded with vegetables. Jaume is particularly keen to show us the difference between two types of preserved anchovies, thin pressed ones from the Basque area in the north of Spain and the fleshier, unpressed l'Escala variety from the north of Catalonia. Then there is a selection of thickly cut artisan cured meats, and local Raf tomatoes with their green striated tops, sliced and slicked with extra-virgin olive oil.

While we perch on stools and sample the foods, he begins making a fish stock from whole rock fish. 'You could just use the bones, but if you use whole fish the stock will taste much better,' he says. This is to be used to make fideua, the main course of our lunch, but it's a long time before

we'll sit down at the dinner table. Jaume wants to play with his gulas, While we were shopping, the fishmonger told him a new way of preparing them. Jaume heats some butter, garlic and dried chilli in a pan, and adds a couple of handfuls of the tiny fish. He fries them ever so briefly before piling them onto serving plates. Then he quickly fries an egg for each person, places them on top of the gulas, which are now white and separate, and drizzles the dishes with a balsamic-style vinegar made in Catalonia. It's delicious. 'Most people in Spain don't eat this dish. We're just having it because the fish were available at the market.' The remaining gulas are placed in a large mixing bowl. Without measuring, Jaume adds flour and an egg yolk and stirs it

together. Then he whisks the white of the egg until frothy and gently folds it in to lighten the lumpy mixture.

'Traditionally, Catalans would use chopped fresh parsley in this dish, but people like me who work in restaurants would be more inclined to use chives to give the mixture a mild garlic flavour.' He then places spoonfuls of the mixture in a hot pan lubricated with oil and cooks them into little fishy pancakes, before placing them on kitchen paper and handing them around. It is as though Jaume is our private chef, dedicated solely to the stimulation of our tastebuds, and before we realise we have stopped eating, he has prepared another new dish for us to taste.

Although dishes are being quickly put together, they are also carefully conceived. Jaume doesn't fry onions like normal people. From his box he pulls out a Ziploc bag filled with beigey brown paste: it is the esteemed and very mild and sweet Figueras onion, sliced and cooked to a marmalade consistency. 'Onions can be cooked in five minutes, but I prefer to cook them for five hours because the onion becomes much sweeter,' he explains. 'You can do a large batch all at once, divide them into portions and keep them in the freezer.' He adds some of the caramelized onion to a frying pan, then carefully folds the excess up in its packet and places it back in the box. 'I keep this because it's like gold' he says.

Truth is, we are full before we even get to the dining table. Jaume's classes are easy-going and flexible, depending on the level of participants' interest. 'Some are really interested and want to improve their cooking and ask questions all the time,' he says. 'Others just listen. Often when we have four people, we find there are two who are really interested and two who just take the classes with them in order to have lunch.' Yet even the less enthusiastic students could not fail to learn something about Barcelona life and Catalan cuisine at one of Jaume Brich's fascinating classes.

Courses currently available

One-week tours including:
Undiscovered Andalusia — Based in Seville, this tour involves tasting wine, olive oils, and local food, visits to local markets and producers, and spend two days cooking traditional dishes. *Catalan Cuisine* — Spend a week touring around Barcelona and viewing its art. Three cookery classes en route will focus on traditional Catalan dishes. Accommodation included.

One-day tours including
The Land of Sherry — Tour the vineyards and see the sherry-making process with a tutored tasting of the different styles of wine. No accommodation included.
The Olive Oil Experience — Visit an olive oil mill with tastings before visiting the nearby village of Zahara de la Sierra. Lunch, included, is a choice of local cheeses and charcuterie meats.

Contact: Culinary Adventures
Viajes Solyma
c/Satunino Calleja, 6
28002 Madrid
Spain
Tel +34 915 316 489 (Madrid)
Tel/Fax +34 932 103 504 (Barcelona)
www.atasteofspain.com

A Question of Taste,
Seville, Spain

Many people think of the potato tortilla as the quintessential Spanish dish, yet it did not — could not — evolve until after the potato was brought to Europe from the Americas in the 16th century. The North African or Moorish influence on Spanish cuisine was exerted long before that, and makes the country's southern region Andalucia one of the most interesting to visit or study. Seville, the area's capital, is renowned as the best place in the country to enjoy tapas bars. Adding to the appeal is the fact that the bodegas of Jerez, and forests with free-roaming black Iberian pigs feeding on acorns, are just short drives away.

Say 'Casablanca' in an English-speaking country and most people think immediately of the Humphrey Bogart-Ingrid Bergman film, rather than the Moroccan city. Say 'Casablanca' in Seville and mouths start watering, for it is the name of what is arguably the best local tapas bar. On the wall, mixed amongst the religious images, newspaper cuttings and photographs of bullfights, is a letter from the office of the King of Spain, who clearly enjoyed his visit. Casablanca is jam-packed every night with Sevillians sharing plates of food and a drink or two. One reason for its distinction is that there is no tapas menu; the dishes available vary daily depending on what the chefs have purchased at the market. It is a difficult place to visit if your Spanish is poor, yet precisely the sort of bar that people generally come to Seville hoping to experience.

Enter Roger Davies, an Englishman who has lived in Spain for several years and spent much of that time working in the local wine industry. He left to set up A Question of Taste, a gastronomic tour company that specializes in Andalucia and offers everything from half-day cooking classes or one-night bar crawls to week-long programmes in which visitors also venture into the countryside to visit cheese, olive oil, ham and sherry producers.

He is visibly relieved that we can all squeeze into a corner with a thin waist-height counter at crowded Casablanca. It's late at night, and it's only Thursday, but the noisy bar has just hit that point at which no one can enter unless someone leaves. Residences in central Seville are so small that there is no culture of entertaining at home, and the numerous tapas bars nearby are effectively off-site annexes of the home. Mind you, this tapas bar doesn't feel particularly spacious either, but that's typical. 'Some bars are almost impossible to get into on Friday or Saturday nights, so during a week-long gastronomic tour we would tend to organize the tapas tour for mid-week on a Wednesday,' Roger explains. 'Whatever the day, however, I only take guests to excellent places that I would like to go to myself.'

LA GIRALDA, THE MOORISH BELL TOWER OF SEVILLE'S CATHEDRAL.

Garbanzos con Espinacas

Like many typically Andalucian dishes, this classic tapas dish of spinach and chickpeas features cumin, a Moorish trait of the region's cuisine. There's another interesting historical attribute too: 'Chickpeas (garbanzos) used to be considered Jewish food in Spain,' says cookery teacher Ruth Roberts, 'and people used to be sent to the Inquisition if they were caught eating them.'

SERVES 6

250 g (8 oz) dried chickpeas (garbanzos)
about 150–175 g (5–6 oz) spinach
2 tablespoons olive oil
3 garlic cloves
1–2 slices day-old bread
1 tablespoon pimenton or sweet paprika
1 teaspoon ground cumin
225 ml (7½ fl oz) (1 cup) chicken or
    vegetable stock
salt

Place the chickpeas (garbanzos) in a bowl, cover generously with water from the tap and leave them to soak overnight, for no more than 12 hours. Drain the chickpeas (garbanzos), discarding the water.

Transfer the chickpeas (garbanzos) to a medium saucepan and cover with fresh water. Bring to a boil, then partly cover the pan with a lid, reduce the heat to a gentle simmer, and cook for 1 hour, or until the chickpeas (garbanzos) are tender. Drain and set aside.

Bring a little water to the boil in the base of a large steamer. Place the spinach in the steaming basket, cover and cook just until the spinach has wilted. Remove from the heat and allow it to cool briefly before using your hands to firmly squeeze the excess water from the spinach. Chop the spinach roughly.

In a large frying pan or skillet, heat a little olive oil. Add the whole garlic cloves and fry them, turning occasionally, until golden. Meanwhile, cube the bread. Remove the garlic from the pan and place in a food processor bowl or large mortar.

Add a little more oil to the pan if necessary, then fry the bread cubes until brown. While the bread is cooking, sprinkle over the pimenton and stir well so that the bread is evenly coated and the spice does not burn. Transfer the contents of the pan to the food processor or mortar. Add the cumin and salt and blend or grind to a paste, gradually adding the stock to make a sauce.

Transfer the sauce to the frying pan, then add the cooked chickpeas (garbanzos) and the chopped cooked spinach. Mix well and allow the mixture to heat through before serving hot.

Roger edges over to the bar to order drinks and find out what's available to eat. He returns with glasses of Manzanilla sherry. 'It's a superb wine to have with tapas. Manzanilla, or Fino, straight from the fridge while preparing dinner is to me one of the most refreshing drinks there is. Even though the best is pricey, it is still a lot cheaper than wines of equivalent quality from other parts of the world.'

When the food is ready, he navigates the crowd to collect it, coming back with a casserole of fresh hake in creamy sauce, a basket of picos bread sticks, the standard though undeniably delicious plate of potato salad, and a dish of curiously grey-brown chunks of juicy meat. We are in for a treat. 'This is carillada, from the face of the pig, which has become quite a popular dish in the last few years,' says Roger, But the meat is too dark to be pork, it looks almost like beef. 'Yes, that's the black Iberian pig, not a regular white pig,' he explains. 'The colour of both the skin and the flesh of the Iberian pig is far darker, and the acorns the animals feed on as they roam the forests around here give the meat an almost nutty flavour.' It is indeed superb.

We move on to El Rinconcillo, the oldest bar in Seville, established in the 1670s and still featuring traditional Moorish brickwork and several designs of intricately patterned tiles. The current owners are the fourth or fifth generation of the same family to run the business. Roger orders glasses of Amontillado

SEVILLE IS FAMOUS FOR ITS TAPAS DISHES.

sherry the colour of mahogany and a plate of finely sliced ham, again the product of Iberian pigs. The meat is flecked with white, somewhat crystalline spots. 'Concentrated amino acids,' Roger explains. 'A good sign that the ham is acorn-fed.' Throughout Spain the Iberian ham is regarded as particularly nutritious. 'They measure the levels of oleic acid in the meat, which have to reach a certain height before the meat is allowed to be classified as acorn-fed ham,' he says.

Next morning cookery teacher Ruth Roberts collects us from the atmospheric Hotel Las Casas de la Judería recommended by Roger and takes us to Seville's central market to buy ingredients for the day's class. An Australian chef who has lived in Spain for many years, she teaches in her gracious apartment

which features a sunny terrace where guests can relax and eat lunch while enjoying views over the cathedral. Today's class will feature several tapas-style dishes; however lessons may instead focus on preparing a typical three-course Andalucian meal. The specific recipes Ruth uses vary according to what is in season, what's good value at the market, and people's areas of interest. She often finds visitors want recipes to take away with them for the famous local Seville oranges, fragrant trees of which line the city's streets, but in fact the Spaniards don't use them much in cooking.

Ruth describes the local cuisine as good, healthy, honest, no-nonsense food. 'People here demand the freshest of everything,' she says. 'A lot of people still shop every day and want the very best.'

Although she wants us to try some ingredients that are unique to the area, her main focus is on dishes people can use back at home. 'I've spent time in the U.S. and England so I know what's available in those countries too. As a teacher, you don't want your students to just enjoy the day and leave it at that.'

She is pleased to see gurmulo — wild spring mushrooms — in the market. These will be used to flavour a revuelto or 'revolved' omelette. The mushrooms are more compact than wild mushrooms often sold elsewhere, yet taste far superior to cultivated varieties.

Aubergines (eggplant) will be used in pezdetierra, which means 'fish of the land' and is a traditional dish for Lent. 'Spain was so poor for so long after the civil war that several non-fish dishes came to be called "fish" so that they could pretend they were eating fish on Fridays,' Ruth explains. She then shows us how she browns the aubergine and garlic in a frying pan in just a little olive oil, so that the vegetable doesn't absorb too much, then it is processed to a nicely speckled paste, adding no more liquid than the oil from the pan in which the aubergine was cooked.

Standing around the central stove, everyone is able to lend a hand with the cooking, though no one has to make a dish from start to finish. We enjoy an aperitif of sherry, then move on to good wine as we sit down to a deliciously varied lunch that exudes the vitality of Andalucia's vibrantly flavoured, vibrantly healthy cuisine.

Courses currently available

Gastronomic Breaks
Four-day tour — Includes olive tasting and a tapas tour in Seville. Accommodation included.
Seven-day tour — Includes trips to local markets, visits to sherry producers and tastings of olive oil. Includes two cooking days and demonstrations. Accommodation included.

Wine Tastings
Featuring wines from Jerez, explanations of how wines are made and how versatile they are with local dishes.

Tapas Tours
A guided tour of the finest tapas bars in Seville.

Customised Tours
Tailormade food and wine tours.
No accommodation included.

Contact: A Question of Taste
Calle Alcázar, 12
41807 Espartinas
Seville
Tel: +34 954.71.37.10
www.aqot.com

Lisa's Kök, Malmö, Sweden

Lisa Forare Winbladh's first cooking job gave her access to the best ingredients Sweden produced. It was something of a shock, therefore, to realize not everyone else in her country ate that well on a daily basis, and as a top-flight food writer she has been helping people to lift their culinary game ever since. On moving to Malmö on the south coast of the country a few years ago, she was thrilled to find a thriving community of specialist gourmet and ethnic food stores. She soon hit upon the idea of offering culinary tours in the area. Cookery classes, held in her funky two-kitchen apartment, were a natural extension. For the local population, sessions are in Swedish but Lisa speaks excellent English, translates well and will conduct English-speaking classes on request.

A small Oriental supermarket crammed with soy sauces, chilli pastes and noodles may not seem the right place to begin an exploration of Swedish cuisine, but Lisa Forare Winbladh's love of food has few borders. Cupping Szechuan peppercorns in her hand, she encourages us to plunge down our noses and inhale deeply. 'What do you smell?' she asks. Errrr... it's, umm, citrussy. 'Citrus? Very good! What type of citrus?' Hmmm — sounds like a trick question, which must mean it's not orange or lemon, so let's say it's lime. 'Lime? Excellent! Wow, you are very good at this.'

No, just good at guessing, but if there's anyone who can make a person feel excited and intrigued about how much they still have to learn about food, it's Lisa. 'Szechuan pepper is a unique tongue-tingling experience and very fashionable in Sweden at the moment,' she continues. 'It has a juniper quality that works very well with game and other Swedish ingredients. Also chocolate. Now smell again. What can you pick up? Do you get those flavours of pine and Christmas spices? That's very much like juniper.'

Szechuan pepper is not the only Oriental ingredient to be making regular appearances in her Swedish dishes. Tubs of deep-fried Asian shallots are one of Lisa's storecupboard staples and she adds them by the handful to meatball mixtures. 'I use them a lot in Swedish cooking because they're so much more aromatic than the fresh Danish shallots we normally get here. Swedish food is very simple so it needs top-quality ingredients to make it work. These are very sweet and simply using them in place of other shallots or onions is an easy way to upgrade your cooking by 10 percent.'

Rummaging through the tall fridges of fresh fruits, vegetables and herbs, she pulls out fresh lemon grass and ginger. 'The first time you taste or smell fresh, good quality lemon grass is like getting your first kiss,' she muses. 'Lemon grass works very nicely with Swedish summer ingredients, and fresh ginger is a good alternative to the dried ginger powder that is very traditional in this country. So at home, I might make a compôte of rhubarb and flavour it with lemon grass and ginger, or with lemon grass and

THE ORESUND BRIDGE — THE 10 MILE LINK BETWEEN COPENHAGEN IN DENMARK AND MALMÖ IN SWEDEN.

vanilla. The marriage of lemon grass and ginger is one made in heaven. You can add them to rhubarb cordial, or a golden plum marmalade. Gravadlax is beautiful made with coarsely grated ginger and finely chopped lemon grass, then served with crème fraîche and lime or wasabi.'

As the culinary ideas spill out of her, Lisa emphasizes that what she's talking about is flavour, not food. 'I make people put their nose right into the ingredient and talk about it in a way that is more commonly associated with wine. Don't be afraid to be ridiculous when you talk about the aromas of food because — honestly — wine people will always say things more ridiculous than you. I believe this is how you should approach all new ingredients, because when you've done

an analysis like this, you know how to use it in the kitchen. Very few chefs do this, which is why fusion cooking so often goes seriously wrong.'

The Swedes use a lot of spices in cooking, though their dishes are not associated with the fiery flavours of Asian countries. Having written a book on spices, Lisa does not expect everyone to keep three different types of coriander seed in the cupboard (Moroccan, Indian and Oriental) as she does, but she encourages people to use them properly. 'The most important thing to learn is to toast spices before using them,' she says. 'It brings out their aromas, makes them less harsh. Swedish people never toast their spices, but you do need to do it.' We move on to Mollans Ost, to sample some of Sweden's best

cheeses and talk about how they are used and served. The Swedish passion for all types of fish is well known, but their delight in combining seafood and cheese is almost unique. The Prastost or Priest's cheese, is thought to go well with pickled herring, while Svarta Malin, which is flavoured with caraway or cumin seeds, is eaten with crayfish. Greve, considered by some to be the Swedish Emmental, is a sweet yet strong cheese. Most impressive — and unsung — however is the skill of this nation in manufacturing high-quality low-fat cheeses, such as Vastan, which has a fat content of only 10 per cent. Before leaving, we try the local cured meats, including Lammkorv, a smoked sausage made not far from Malmö airport, and a smoked ham from Oland, a small island just off the coast.

Wild Meatballs with Roast Parsnips, Browned Butter and Toasted Juniper

SERVES 4

FOR THE MEATBALLS

2 slices stale white bread

1/3 teaspoon ground allspice

2/3 teaspoon thyme

1/2 teaspoon freshly ground black pepper

2 teaspoon brown sugar

2 teaspoon salt

5 tablespoons light cream, half and half, or milk

500 g (1 lb 2 oz) minced deer or venison

a little vegetable oil

2 tablespoons butter

FOR THE PARSNIPS

4 medium parsnips

2 tablespoons butter

FOR THE SPICED BUTTER SAUCE

50 g (2 oz) (1/4 cup) butter

2 tablespoons finely chopped shallots

1 teaspoon crushed juniper berries

50 ml (2 fl oz) (1/4 cup) water

1 tablespoon stock concentrate

1 tablespoon sherry vinegar

'This is a delightfully simple sauce with few ingredients, yet utterly sophisticated flavours,' says Lisa. 'Toasting gives the pungent juniper berries milder, nuttier aromas.' It is essential to work the meatball mixture carefully. 'Too little and it crumbles, too much and the meatballs turn out dry,' she says.

Trim the crusts from the white bread and tear the bread into small pieces. Place in a large mixing bowl, sprinkle with the allspice, thyme, sugar and salt, then pour over the cream or milk and leave to soak for about 15 minutes.

Add the minced meat to the soaked bread and work together to give a smooth mixture. Leave to mature in the fridge for 1 hour – this makes the meatballs juicier as the salt in the mixtures works as a brine.

Meanwhile, prepare the roast parsnips. Preheat the oven to 200°C (400°F) Gas 6. Trim and peel the parsnips, then cut them lengthwise in four wedges. Heat the butter in a frying pan. Add the parsnips and fry over a high heat until lightly golden. Transfer the vegetables to an ovenproof dish and continue baking in the oven for 30 minutes or until tender.

To make the butter sauce, gently heat the butter in a saucepan with the shallots and juniper berries and fry until the shallots are golden brown and fragrant. Add the water, stock and vinegar. Simmer gently for a few minutes, then set aside in a warm place.

To finish the meatballs, wash your hands and rub them with some oil. Take even-sized portions of the mixture and roll them into balls of about 3 cm (1 inch) in diameter. Make as many as you can with the mixture and place them on an oiled plate. Heat the butter in a frying pan and fry the meatballs over a medium heat until they are golden brown and barely pink in the middle. Serve with the roast parsnips, spooning the spiced butter sauce over the vegetables.

Lisa is particular about where she shops for her classes, so we visit an Eastern European butcher in order to buy mince for our meatballs. 'For Swedish meatballs you need very good quality mince. This is the best you can find because it is just taken from the leg of pork and is therefore very lean,' she explains. 'I also like this shop because they have a cut called "false goose thigh" that is the tenderest part of the front leg. It is traditional in Eastern Europe and also popular here.'

ONE OF SWEDEN'S MANY WINDMILL ATTRACTIONS.

Then it's on to the game shop where the array of meat products would challenge even die-hard carnivores, let alone anyone with fluffy bunny syndrome. We see smoked beaver, moose and rooster as well as wild boar, deer and veal. There is also gravadlax made from reindeer. 'In spring they have very tender black birds that are a speciality of this area, like a spring chicken but with more flavour,' says Lisa.

Before starting as a cooking teacher and food-tour operator, Lisa took a lot of cookery classes herself. 'One of the reasons I decided to do this was because I wasn't very happy with them,' she reveals. 'My classes are like workshops. They are interactive. You don't just sit back and watch a chef.' She finds that teaching in a home kitchen makes people more relaxed. A typical class would comprise eight to ten people who together would cook and eat seven or eight dishes over five hours. 'A cavalcade of dishes. Some of them we make up on the spot. It can get pretty chaotic,' she admits. 'I like to teach people food that can be prepared in advance so people can entertain at home easily. The dishes are very simple but with sophisticated flavours. Chef schools are all very elegant but the dishes they teach require you to spend too much time in the kitchen.' Ironically, learning these simple and easy ways with food via Lisa is likely to make you want to spend more time in the kitchen too.

LEFT: THE MARKET AT MOLLEVANGEN.

ABOVE: CLOUDBERRIES, OFTEN USED IN SWEDISH DISHES.

This one-day course is currently the only course Lisa offers.

Involves hands-on cooking and demonstrations as well as tours around local specialist food stores. No accommodation included.

Contact: Lisa's Kök
Hantverkangatan 16
SE-2 11 55 Malmo
Sweden
Tel: +46 (0)40 123 624

The Oriental, Bangkok, Thailand

Standing on the lush yet pristine patio of The Oriental Thai Cooking School, edging under the banana trees to escape the intense midday light, it's easy to see why exotic dishes just don't taste the same when made at home. We chew on leaves from verdant pots of mild, sweet and strong basils, then sniff roots of galangal, ginger and gra chai (the 'lesser' galangal), each of which are carefully chosen by Thai cooks to produce subtly different effects in their dishes. Even the most sophisticated supermarkets at home suddenly seem to offer nothing but a gross over-generalisation of 'authentic' products. Ginger is not for curries — its strong flavour is reserved for stir-fries of meat and seafood. Curries need galangal. The celery's different, the broccoli's different, there are myriad varieties of aubergine (eggplant) and cucumber. No wonder this school has no compunction in offering four days of classroom-style tuition to help visitors grasp the important cultural and culinary aspects of Thailand's fascinatingly diverse range of ingredients.

OPPOSITE: THE BEST FLOATING MARKET IS AT DAMNOEN SADUAK, ABOUT AN HOUR'S DRIVE FROM BANGKOK.

'Don't be polite. Kill it! Like this!' Instructor Krissanapong Kiattisak, or Kris as we are invited to call him, takes the knife and whacks it down forcefully on a coriander (cilantro) root about to ascend to culinary heaven, taking its rightful place in a dish of Kaow Soi Kai (chicken curry with egg noodles). This is day five of the Thai cooking course run by the prestigious Oriental hotel in Bangkok, and the first of two days in which students venture from classroom-style instruction to hands-on cooking.

With the size of hands-on sessions limited to eight, guests work in small groups concentrating on ingredient preparation techniques rather than churning out dishes. For those with experience of Thai or other Asian cooking, these classes may seem a little rudimentary, but to a beginner who has done nothing more than reheat a Thai-style ready-meal, or someone who's never attended a cooking class before, this programme is achievable and confidence-boosting. Importantly, participants can dip in and out of the course as desired. There is no requirement to sign up for the full six days, so if your visit to Bangkok only allows one or two mornings for cooking classes, you can still join in the sessions.

Kris is not as ruthless with seafood as he is with coriander. When talking the class through a dish of stir-fried curry crab, he introduces the fresh, live crustacean essential to make the dish and admits that when it comes to killing crab he's, well, chicken. Sompop, his expert assistant chef and star of the fruit-carving sessions, takes it to the back room for dispatch.

Throughout the sessions Sompop and kitchen staff from the hotel discreetly tidy up and offer tips, encouragement and

ORIGINAL BUILDING IS NOW 'THE AUTHOR'S WING'.

Drunken Noodles

SERVES 2

30 g (1 oz) kale

1 large fresh red chilli, thinly sliced

¼ long red pepper, thinly sliced

15 g (½ oz) gra chai or lesser galangal

½ medium tomato, sliced

45 g (1½ oz) white fish fillet

45 g (1½ oz) fresh raw green shrimp
   or prawns

30 g (1 oz) fresh raw scallop meat

30 g (1 oz) fresh raw squid

4 tablespoons vegetable oil

4–6 raw clams

4–6 raw mussels

130 g (4½ oz) fresh wide Thai rice noodles

2 tablespoons oyster sauce

1 tablespoon fish sauce

1 teaspoon white sugar

a bunch of holy basil, about 15 g (½ oz),
   trimmed (alternatively use basil mixed
   with a little ground black pepper)

¼ teaspoon freshly ground black pepper

a few sprigs of fresh young green
   peppercorns (optional)

Known as Guay Teaw Phad Khee Mao, this hot, spicy dish of stir-fried rice noodles is a popular morning-after breakfast in Thailand. You are supposed to add one chilli for every glass of wine you drank — so you feel more pain from the chilli than the alcohol. Just cooking it wakes you up, such is the aroma, but it can get smoky so watch the fire alarm. Choy sum or broccoli can be used in place of the kale. If desired, you can use leftover cooked rice (from the night before) instead of the noodles, and garnish with deep-fried basil leaves. Alternatively, omit the noodles, add some water to give a gravy, and serve on top of plain boiled rice.

To prepare the kale, use a vegetable peeler to peel the base of the stems. Remove the leaves and cut them into ribbons. Thinly slice the base of the vegetable on the diagonal. Set aside.

Thinly slice the large red chilli and the red pepper. Peel the gra chai and slice lengthways before cutting again to give long thin julienne strips. Set the chilli, red pepper and gra chai aside in a bowl, separate from the kale.

Slice the tomato into thin wedges and set aside separately.

Cut the white fish into strips. Peel the shrimp, discarding the heads and tails, then run a small sharp knife around the back of the shrimp. Lift out and discard the black intestinal thread.

Leave the scallop meat whole if small, otherwise cut it into thick discs. Slice the squid and set aside with the rest of the prepared seafood.

Heat 2 tablespoons of the vegetable oil in a wok over a moderate heat. When the oil is hot, add the fish, shrimp, scallop meat, squid, mussels and clams. Stir-fry for 2 minutes or until the seafood is almost cooked. Remove to a plate and set aside.

Add the remaining 2 tablespoons of vegetable oil to the wok and stir-fry the rice noodles for 2 minutes or until they are almost cooked. Then add the prepared kale and stir-fry for another minute or so.

Return the seafood to the wok and stir-fry until well-combined with the noodles and kale. Season with the oyster sauce, fish sauce and white sugar.

Add the red chilli, red pepper and lesser galangal, and stir-fry briefly. Then stir in the tomato, holy basil, black pepper and fresh green peppercorns (if using). Quickly remove from the heat and serve.

plenty of hands-on help. The guests, who have a diverse range of abilities, come from countries such as the U.S., Germany, Australia and Britain. It's not essential to stay at The Oriental in order to participate in its cookery classes, though it's such a glorious old establishment — Bangkok's first hotel — most people want to. Each day begins with a bumpy trip across the Chao Phraya, the city's 'river of kings', on the hotel's fun and efficient shuttle boat service. The classes take place in a leafy facility opposite the residences. This also houses the Oriental's world-renowned spa, gym and traditional Thai restaurant, the Sala Rim Naam.

Although the Thais cook with woks, there are several differences between the way they are used in Thailand and China. Most notably, the material of choice for the pan is brass, and the traditional Chinese wok scoop is ignored in favour of tools made from coconut wood, which don't scratch the metal. In the semi-industrial kitchen at the rear of the school's lecture area, the wok burners are set about mid-thigh. 'The low height is good for stir-frying because it allows you to see over the wok,' Kris explains. 'We'll have to redesign our kitchens,' quips one guest. It certainly makes stir-frying seem easier. So does the habit of using two wok scoops to move the ingredients around the pan.

Throughout the sessions, Kris constantly advises on the best substitutes to use should the authentic product not be readily available at home. 'Fresh coconut

has the best smell and sweetness but it's a lot of job.' He lifts up a sizable block of wood, the size of a child's bench, carved into the shape of a gigantic rabbit. It has a spiked metal plate emerging from its nose. 'In Thai homes, this is used to carve the meat from the coconut shell,' he says. 'It's called a "rabbit", but these days they come in other shapes too, such as crocodiles and horses and are something of a collector's item. The animals help motivate children to grate the coconut, otherwise it's men's work.'

In Thailand it is often possible to buy ready-grated fresh coconut meat from the markets but, says Kris, the UHT packets of coconut cream are very good. 'I would always choose that over a can, it's much better. If you do have to use canned coconut milk, don't shake it. Scoop the coconut cream from the top of the can and stir-fry it with the oil and flavourings at the beginning of cooking, until it is aromatic and starts to exude its natural oil. Then add the rest of the coconut "milk" later in the making of the dish. If you add the entire can all at once you won't get the right result.'

None of the actual cooking is complicated; it's the preparation of the herbs and spices that entails the most work. Heavy granite mortars and pestles are used for grinding the famous Thai curry pastes, and this also is considered men's work, says Kris. He cuts open a dried serrano chilli with scissors to remove the seeds, then snips it into smaller pieces and

TWO-HANDELLED BRASS WOKS ARE FAVOURED FOR COOKING IN THAILAND. THEY ARE ATTRACTIVE, BUT IT IS TIME-CONSUMING TO KEEP THEM LOOKING SMART.

soaks it in warm water for five minutes to make it easier to pound. 'You need to pound the chilli until it's very fine before you add any of the other ingredients, because it is the hardest thing to get fine.'

It turns out Kris and Sompop have slightly different techniques for successful grinding. Kris pounds straight up and down most of the time, while turning the mortar regularly with his free hand; Sompop tends to work the ingredients more round the sides of the granite bowl. As he demonstrates his preferred method, he lifts his head up to reveal glistening eyes. 'The fumes make me cry,' he laughs, 'I have to keep my head back.'

Ready-made curry pastes are not rejected entirely. Kris suggests 'waking up' commercial brands with the addition of a little grilled shrimp paste and some

lemon grass. 'Add it to the ready-made curry paste and pound again. It means the dish takes 15 minutes to make rather than an hour.' He provides simple instructions for making 'magic paste', a combination of pounded coriander root, garlic and pepper. 'It's good for almost everything,' he says, 'but especially grilled or steamed seafood.'

The important thing to remember when using coriander in Thai recipes is that, should the strongly flavoured roots be unavailable, it is necessary to double the quantity of leaf and stalk to compensate. 'We often slice the stems thinly and use them as a garnish,' Kris adds.

He recommends a visit to the Chatuchak Weekend Market at Morchit for buying Thai ingredients and equipment, and experiencing something of real Bangkok life. While it's a fair distance from the rarefied Oriental, the trip is easy and quick thanks to the shuttle boat service and modern skytrain. Thailand's most famous floating markets are at Damnoen Saduak, about an hour's drive from Bangkok, and although increasingly commercialized, they are worth a visit. Daily excursions operate from the city and can be arranged through most hotels.

Nearby hotels The Peninsula and The Shangri-La also offer Thai cooking classes. For The Peninsula tel: +66 (0)2 861 2888 or email slaoharanu@peninsula.com. For The Shangri-La tel: +66 (0)2 236 7777. A more homely experience can be had at the Baipai Thai Cooking School, endorsed by the Ministry of Education. Set in a residential area of Bangkok, the price includes transfers to and from hotels in the centre of the city. Visit www.baipai.com for further details.

THE STREET FOOD STALLS NEAR THE ORIENTAL HOTEL ARE SOME OF THE CITY'S MOST INVITING.

Courses currently available

4-day course or half-day of your choice from:
Monday: Intro, ingredients, snacks and salads
Tuesday: Soups, desserts, fruit & vegetable carvings
Wednesday: Curries, condiments, and side dishes
Thursday: Steam, stir fry, fry and grilled dishes
Onsite accommodation is optional.

Contact: The Oriental
Thai Cooking School
48 Oriental Avenue
Bangkok 10500
Tel +66 (0)2 437 3080
Fax +66 (0)2 439 7587
www.mandarinoriental.com

Lanna Cooking School,
Chiang Mai, Thailand

Thailand is now chock full of interesting cookery courses to suit all pockets, but the blue ribbon for the most stunning location has to go to the Lanna Cooking School at the Four Seasons Resort in Chiang Mai. Surrounded by serenely misty tree-covered mountains, the new facility has been inspired by traditional northern Thai buildings and is a pleasing combination of rustic equipment and modern services. Take the chopping boards — there's none of that polypropylene or fused end-grain stuff, just thick hunks of solid tamarind tree trunk. The mixing bowls are all gorgeous turned teak wood. Heck, even the placemats could make your mouth water. Lanna, the traditional name of the region around Chiang Mai, means 'million rice paddies' and the Four Seasons, which features a rice paddy at its centre, is in Mae Rim Valley, a 30 minute drive from the city's international airport.

First we pray. The spirit house outside the Lanna Cooking School contains miniature figures of a grandfather and grandmother. We know they are old because they have grey hair and are wearing very thick glasses. Every day they receive offerings of food and water to keep them happy in the hope that they will in turn bless the school. On special occasions they get whisky. Incense sticks are set alight and each person takes a bundle of nine (a lucky number in Thailand) to hold as they say a brief prayer. It's the kind of ritual you may expect to be put on to charm the tourists but in fact it happens even when no one has booked a class.

The Lanna Cooking School can take up to eight students (they'll sometimes squeeze in nine) for its hands-on sessions, though the number can vary substantially from one day to the next. Classes run six days

a week and the subjects are organized into stand-alone units that can be taken individually or combined to cover the gamut of Thai cooking in line with guests' personal interests and holiday schedule.

Head teacher Chef Pritak demonstrates each dish before participants go to their personal workstations to try it themselves, then sit down to sample their efforts. The half-day sessions culminate in a full meal of the food cooked that morning, served on the terrace. Optional extras include an early morning visit to a food market in Chiang Mai, and a fruit and vegetable carving session.

Pritak teaches in English but encourages people to use the Thai names of dishes and ingredients as much as possible. 'If you go into a Thai restaurant and ask for a spicy beef salad, there are lots of dishes

LABOURERS WALKING THROUGH THE MAE RIM VALLEY ON THEIR WAY TO WORK AT THE REGENT HOTEL.

ABOVE: KING PRAWNS AND RICE NOODLES ARE A
THAI SPECIALITY.

RIGHT: THE HOMELY KITCHENS OF THE LANNA
COOKING SCHOOL.

they could bring you, but if you ask for Yum Nua, they will know exactly the one you want.' It's the same with ingredients such as chilli sauces, of which there are several different styles including Narm Prig Paow, Prik Srilacha and Nam Yum.

Having worked for several years in the Middle East and Europe, Pritak is practised at recommending reliable substitutes for some of the more specialized ingredients. Who would have thought kohlrabi or cucumber was the best alternative to green papaya? Or that carrot or cabbage could be used in place of banana blossom? Ducks' gizzards and pigs' blood are among some of the more unusual ingredients employed, but many of the dishes could easily be made at home after a trip to an Oriental

supermarket. Quite a lot of pre-preparation is done for the participants, from weighing and measuring to deep-frying a series of crispy flavourings, but some of the typically unfamiliar items such as banana blossom are left to be tackled and each person cooks and finishes each dish themselves.

Everyone has a go at making egg nets around a central burner, the tabletop covered with banana leaves to catch the ensuing mess. Pritak favours a mix of chicken and duck eggs, the latter bringing extra colour and viscosity to the batter. Although a shiny new Teflon pan is used in preference to a wok for cooking the net, a rustic bundle of bamboo skewers is favoured for spreading the batter. The trick we all struggle with is moving

Yum Nua

According to Pritak, the Thais believe that eating five cloves of pickled garlic every day will make you strong. This versatile dressing is spicy, sour, sweet and salty and can be served with steamed fish, or barbecued seafood, chicken or pork, or cellophane noodles. You could use a food processor to make the dressing but the result won't be quite as fragrant because the ingredients would be finely chopped rather than crushed as they are in a mortar. It is definitely worth barbecuing the beef if possible as the smoky charred flavour enhances the dish. In Thailand this salad would be garnished with flowers shaped from fresh red chillies.

SERVES 2

200 g (7 oz) beef sirloin, trimmed
salt and freshly ground black pepper
2 handfuls mixed lettuce leaves
2 tomatoes
1 mild onion
½ cucumber
a few mint sprigs
4 spring onions, green parts only

FOR THE SAUCE

2 coriander (cilantro) roots
4 cloves garlic
1 fresh red chilli, about 5–7.5 cm
   (2–3 inches)
10 red or green bird's eye chillies
2 teaspoons white sugar
10 cloves Thai pickled garlic
6 tablespoons mushroom soy sauce
6 tablespoons lime juice

Preheat a ridged grill pan, chargrill or barbecue. Season the steak with salt and pepper. Grill for 2–3 minutes on each side according to the meat's thickness and the desired degree of doneness. Remove from the heat and set the steak aside to rest.

To make the sauce, roughly chop the coriander root and garlic and place in a mortar. Pound until they start to break down. Slice the red chilli and bird's eye chillies and add to the mortar. Keep pounding until the mixture begins to form a paste. Add the sugar and pickled garlic and crush again, then use the pestle to stir in the mushroom soy sauce and lime juice.

Arrange the lettuce leaves on serving plates. Slice the tomato, onion and cucumber and divide them between the plates. Slice the beef and place on top. Spoon the sauce over, then garnish with the mint and spring onions.

Serve within 1 hour.

outside the imagined boundary of the
pan. Egg nets work best when you
swoosh the batter right over the edges
and onto the table before sweeping back
in the other direction. Even with the
banana leaves in place and permission to
go crazy, we all make the brush hover
right over the frying pan, so that the
batter collects in puddles in the corners.
Result: we are neat, the egg nets are not.

Making Kaow Ob Sapporod, the famous
dish of pineapple stuffed with curried
rice, Chinese sausage and prawns, it is
amusing to see how Brits and Canadians
react when Pritak scoops perfectly ripe,
heavenly juicy pineapple straight from
the shell and into the bin. 'Ahhhh! You
can't waste that!' He shrugs. 'Pineapple
here is not very expensive. We only need

BAMBOO RIVER RAFTING IN CHIANG MAI.

a little bit for the filling.' It's not the only cultural difference. The Westerners love the nutty taste and firm texture of the local wholegrain rices but Pritak screws up his nose and smiles. 'Brown rice is high in calcium and good for your bones but Thais generally like soft rice.'

The noodle class begins with a tasting of the many fresh and dried products used in Thai cooking, with advice on preparation, cooking and possible substitutes. Fresh rice noodles taste markedly better than their dried counterparts, but the most important thing we learn is that — despite what the packet might state — for stir-fries the dried noodles do not have to be rehydrated in advance of cooking. The pan will contain enough moisture to soften them perfectly. It's a long way to travel for such a simple tip, yet it's the sort of helpful, results-transforming clarification that makes it very worthwhile.

To book courses at Lanna Cooking School ontact Gourmet on Tour (see right).

Other courses in Thailand

The Boathouse — Based at the beach resort of Phuket, this hotel and restuarant offer four-day hands-on Thai cooking classes, held regularly from April to October. Accommodation is included.

Contact: Gourmet on Tour
Berkeley Square House
2F Berkeley Square
Mayfair
London W1J 6BD
Tel UK +44 (0)20 7396 5550
Fax UK +44 (0)20 7900 1527
Tel US 1 800 504 9842
Fax US 1 800 886 2229
www.gourmetontour.com

The Culinary Institute of America, New York, USA

The majesty of The Culinary Institute of America's Hudson River Valley campus, with its sweeping parkland and water views, and distinguished buildings, brings a sense of gravitas to its purpose — teaching people to cook. A not-for-profit organisation, it is the only residential college in the world devoted to culinary education and in addition to training 2,000 undergraduates and 6,000 professionals per annum, welcomes the general public to weekend classes and workshops, some demonstration-only, some hands-on. In recent years the CIA has also pioneered the field of online culinary education, demonstrating the dynamic and forward-thinking nature of this thriving school.

'Come in, sit down. You're late. You'll have to stay after class and drink wine.' Lecturer Bill Guilfoyle's sense of humour is as dry as a bottle of Muscadet. Like anyone's favourite professor from college days, he combines the formality of institutionalized education with the irreverence of someone determined to enjoy their job. Fortunately for him, wine and food are a large part of his occupation. 'You know, I started tasting wine seriously 30 years ago and I still learn something every day,' he says. 'It's like golf. But I'm not going to tell you this wine has hints of lingonberries and frog's urine or things like that, because this course is meant to be fun.'

Today's session on wine and food pairing is just one of several courses offered by the CIA at weekends for enthusiastic amateurs. The programme, which attracts about 1,600 people each year, takes in cuisines such as Puerto Rican, Floribbean, Soul Food and Low Country cooking, Japanese, Indian, even Polish. Classical culinary techniques are covered in classes such as Stocks and Sauces, Pâtés and Terrines, Basic Butchery and Sharpening Your Knife Skills. There are courses for people who just love a particular style of food or cooking — such as Cookies and Brownies, or Grilling and Smoke Roasting — as well as those who want to prepare for specific challenges such as cocktail parties, wedding receptions and running a B&B. And if you just can't shake off that dream of opening your own restaurant, there are five-day intensive Boot Camps and Career Discovery programmes to help you assess whether you've got what it takes.

A former chef, restaurateur and sommelier, Bill is a leadling local restaurant critic and teaches in the CIA bachelor's degree programme. 'Just knowing how to cook is not enough to make it in this industry anymore,' he says. 'CIA graduates work everywhere from Cheesecake Factory to Thomas Keller's French Laundry. We prepare them for work in corporate life or independent restaurants and teach everything, including how to repair their

Chocolate Polenta Soufflé

400 ml (13 fl oz) (1¾ cups) milk

1 large strip orange zest

55 g (2 oz) (¼ cup) cornmeal

2 tablespoons unsweetened cocoa powder

85 g (13 oz) (½ cup) caster sugar,
  plus extra for dusting

40 g (1½ oz) bittersweet chocolate

a little butter, for greasing

4 large egg whites

sifted icing sugar (confectioners' sugar),
  to decorate

Adpated from the Culinary Institute of America's ground-breaking Techniques of Healthy Cooking course, this surprising recipe uses cornmeal porridge as a low-fat base for a satisfyingly rich-tasting soufflé. Chocolate is famously tough to pair with wine and as Bill Guilfoyle's class reveals, results can vary based on whether the chocolate used is semi-sweet or bittersweet.

Place the milk and orange zest in a large, heavy saucepan. Bring to a boil, then remove from the heat and set aside to infuse for 30 minutes. Discard the zest.

Return the milk to a simmer and gradually whisk in the cornmeal and cocoa powder, beating constantly to avoid lumps. Set aside 2 tablespoons of the caster sugar for whisking into the egg whites, and whisk the remaining sugar into the saucepan.

Reduce the heat to a very gentle simmer and cook, stirring often, for 25 minutes or until the mixture is thick and rich. Remove from the heat and grate the chocolate into the pan. Stir to combine, then set aside to cool.

Grease four 225 ml (7½ fl oz) (1 cup) ramekins or soufflé dishes. Place some extra caster sugar in one and gently shake it round the inside of the dish to line it with a thin crust of crystals. Tap out the excess sugar and repeat with the remaining dishes.

When the chocolate mixture has cooled, preheat the oven to 200°C (400°F) Gas Mark 6. In a large and very clean bowl, preferably copper, stainless steel or toughened glass, whisk the egg whites until soft peaks form. Add the reserved 2 tablespoons of sugar and whisk until the whites form a stiff, glossy meringue.

Take a large spoonful of meringue and stir it into the chocolate mixture to help lighten it. Then repeat with another spoonful of meringue.

Gently fold the chocolate mixture into the bowl of meringue, carefully cutting and stirring the mixture until it is well combined, without squashing out the air bubbles in the meringue.

Divide the soufflé mixture between the prepared dishes and place them together in a baking dish. Fill the baking dish with water until the level reaches two-thirds up the sides of the soufflé dishes. Bake for 25 minutes until risen, then serve hot, dusted with icing sugar.

own equipment.' Interestingly, only 30 per cent of CIA graduates choose to stay in the industry over the course of their entire careers. It's tough out there.

The CIA was funded in 1946 as the New Haven Restaurant Institute in Connecticut with the aim of providing job training for World War II veterans, and was renamed the Culinary Institute of America in 1952 to reflect its national student population. It moved to Hyde Park, New York, in 1972, taking over the Jesuit seminary of St-Andrew-on-Hudson and that same year was granted a charter by the state of New York to confer associates degrees in culinary arts. Recognising the emerging importance of the West Coast in the food and wine industry, the CIA opened its Greystone campus in the Napa Valley in 1995. Although it is a stunning and well-appointed destination for culinary

professionals, the no-less-attractive Hudson River Valley campus offers the better range of classes for amateur cooks, whether adults or children.

Bill's class in wine and food pairing is divided between the Institute's Wine Spectator lecture theatre, where the theory is explained, and the CIA's American Bounty restaurant, where the theory is put into practice. The campus features four restaurants and a bakery-café, all staffed by students and open to the general public. Not surprisingly, the Escoffier restaurant specialising in classic French cuisine was the first to open, but the CIA soon appreciated the growing status of new American cuisine and opened a second fine dining venue — American Bounty — to reflect the trend. Here we enjoyed dishes such as Alaskan king salmon rolls with Chinese-style

LEFT: FRUIT TARTLETS.

RIGHT: MIXING CHOCOLATE IN CLASS.

OPPOSITE LEFT: SHIRLEY CHENG TEACHES THE
'ASIAN CUISINE' CLASS IN WHICH STUDENTS LEARN
BASIC KNIFE SKILLS.

OPPOSITE RIGHT: TYPICAL CLASSES AT THE CIA PROVIDE
EXCELLENT FACILITIES AND AMPLE SPACE FOR STUDENTS.

vegetables and ponzu dipping sauce, and a bacon-wrapped pork loin with duck tamale and an orange and sarsaparilla sauce. Whether or not they matched the fine wines selected was for us to decide.

'We're going to make Riesling fans of you today,' Bill announces. It seems to go with nearly everything and, when drunk alongside the fiery spiciness of the salmon dish in particular, acts as a salve for the palate. No wonder it is recommended in so many Asian restaurants. Also, with an alcohol content of just 7.5 per cent 'you can drink a lot of it and not get hammered', as Bill jokes. Pinot Grigio, on the other hand, seems to amplify the spiciness of the salmon.

BAKING BREAD IN THE COLLEGE BAKESHOP.

Rosé was one of the options presented with the main course. Although generally underrated, it is a very adaptable choice of wine for dining and worked well with the orange and sarsaparilla sauce. 'People often think they need to match the wine to the protein in the dish but the sauce can change everything,' says Bill. So too can the main cooking method — a poached or steamed fish will have a very different effect in the mouth from the same species when it has been coated in spices and blackened as in Cajun cooking.

There are two basic choices, says Bill; to select wine to complement the food, which is a simple pairing, or to pick a wine that contrasts with it, which is more fun, or risky, depending on how you look at it. 'Contrasting takes the various flavours of the dish and adds another flavour of wine to create something even better.' Well, that's the theory. Fortunately we can have a good time trying to put it into practice.

Other professional classes

The California Culinary Academy in San Francisco is a professional school offering Saturday classes for enthusiastic home cooks with some of the Bay Area's leading chefs.

See www.baychef.com for details.

Courses currently available

Enthusiasts — One-day hands-on courses including:
The Joy of Healthy Cuisine — Learn to create delicious meals while lowering cholesterol and strengthening hearts and the immune system.
Timeless Desserts — Learn how to produce professional looking and tasting desserts and sauces.
Pastry Basics — Learn the basics to baking everyone's favourites, whether seasonal pies or cookies, cakes and brownies.

Enthusiasts — Two-day hands-on courses including:
Flavour Dynamics — Learn how to make food taste good, what flavour is, and how it can be applied to food or developed from ingredients already there.

Other Enthusiasts programmes include:
Demonstrations; Kids in the Kitchen; Boot Camp; Career Discovery and Travel Programmes.

Contact: Culinary Institute of America
1946 Campus Drive
Hyde Park
New York 12538
USA
Tel +1 845 452 9600
www.ciachef.edu

Santa Fe School of Cooking, New Mexico, USA

Set on the first floor of a small shopping centre in the heart of old Sante Fe, the Sante Fe School of Cooking specializes in traditional and contemporary cuisine of the American southwest. Most classes are demonstration-only, taking place in the teaching kitchen-cum-dining room behind the well-stocked colourful shop at the front of the premises. The published programme includes classes such as Traditional New Mexican I, II and III, Southwest Vegetarian, Southwest Breakfast, Fajitas, Cuisines of Mexico and Mexican Light — a varied selection that shows the clear focus of the school. Nearby hotel The Inn on the Alameda offers attractive packages that include a cooking class, two nights' accommodation and a discount meal at the popular local restaurant Ristra.

LEFT: CHILLI RISTRAS ARE SEEN HANGING OUTSIDE MANY BUILDINGS IN SANTE FE, EVEN GALLERIES AND BOUTIQUES.

RIGHT: THE INN ON THE ALAMEDA OFFERS CLASS-AND-ACCOMMODATION PACKAGES WITH THE COOKING SCHOOL.

Lois Ellen Frank is one of several food experts to teach regularly at the Sante Fe School of Cooking, but fresh from her win of a James Beard Award for her book *Foods of the Southwest Indian Nations* (the first time a book on indigenous American food has been recognized by the James Beard Foundation), she is perhaps also the most prestigious.

A professional chef, successful photographer, and culinary anthropologist who has spent much time investigating the use of corn throughout the American continent, she is now working on her PhD, preparing a thesis on how (and why) contemporary chefs use indigenous ingredients. Lois admits that her menu for the day's class had to be altered slightly so that not every single dish included corn, but her enthusiasm for it is infectious, and the subject quickly becomes fascinating as she describes the many varieties of corn and corn products, and their cultural, religious and culinary significance.

The yellow sweetcorn cooked and served on the cob as a fresh vegetable is but part of the story. There are also white, blue (really almost black), red and speckled varieties, ground into meals, or dried and processed with ash to produce posole or hominy, or roasted in an adobe oven to make chicos.

Like the indigenous cooks she has studied so carefully, Lois has developed the habit of letting nothing go to waste. The skins from the ears of corn she has peeled are turned into plate decorations and used to tie the legs of quails during roasting; the stripped corn cobs are added to the stock pot, (once their flavour is extracted can then be used to comfort teething babies); the seedy central core of a julienned courgette (zucchini) is kept for soup making; day-old bread is employed in stuffing, and is the better for its

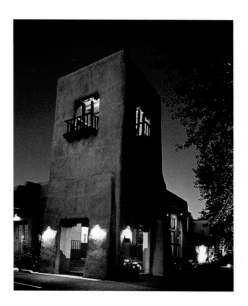

WATERMELONS FRESH FROM THE FARM IN NEW MEXICO.

staleness. 'The whole essence of native cooking is to use every piece of everything,' says Lois.

Indeed, honouring what nature provides seems to be an important theme. 'Native people did what I call "acceptance farming". Foods grew wild, and yet they were cultivated, because people interracted with them to make them produce more. The plants thrived on this interaction. The native people would leave some of the produce for other creatures so they could eat to survive too. This helped to ensure the food supply.'

Lois begins her demonstration with a chocolate cake made from pine nuts (known as piñons locally), silky blue cornmeal, eggs and vanilla. 'Piñons are extremely important to this region,' she says. 'They are high in calories but nutritionally significant, especially in times of famine. Unfortunately at the moment there is a piñon blight. The drought has compromised the trees and we are looking at losing up to 80 per cent of the crop.'

Traditionally, a variety of ingredients would be routinely stored to protect people against hard times. Nuts, seeds, beans and grain could be stored for years, and the handcrafted pots that make such attractive souvenirs for Sante Fe's tourists today owe their shape to the clever traditional technique of protecting these stored ingredients from rodents by curving the sides of the pot sharply and making just a tiny opening in the top of the container.

Not everything in the class is traditional, however. 'Here is my contemporary grinding stone,' says Lois, lifting up a

Spicy Corn Soup

Lois Ellen Frank admits that the cream in this substantial yet elegant soup is a chef's touch in the tradition of refined French cooking. 'Made without cream, this soup is as traditional as you can get, but the cream makes it silky,' she says.

SERVES 6

4 corn cobs
1 tablespoon olive oil
1 onion, chopped
1 tablespoon crushed garlic
1 tablespoon dried chipotle chilli powder
1.35 litres (2¼ pints) (6 cups) chicken stock
1 teaspoon salt
½ teaspoon freshly ground black pepper
225 ml (7½ fl oz) (1 cup) double cream
2–4 tablespoons sauce from jar of
   chipotle in adobe sauce (optional)

FOR THE SAUCE

1 red bell pepper
125 ml (4 fl oz) (½ cup) double cream

Preheat the oven to 180°C (350°F) Gas Mark 4. Wash the corn cobs and place them unpeeled in a baking tray. Pour in enough water to come 1.5cm (¾ inch) up the sides of the tin. Transfer the tray of corn to the hot oven and steam-roast for 10 minutes, turning the corn halfway through cooking.

While the corn is cooking, put the red bell pepper in a separate pan and place it in the oven. Roast for 20 minutes, or until the skin blisters and chars.

When the corn is done, remove it from the oven, lift the cobs from the water and allow to cool briefly. Peel away and discard the skins and silks. Holding each cob upright on a chopping board, cut the kernels away from the cobs and set aside, Then chop each corn cob into two or three pieces and set aside.

Heat the olive oil in a large saucepan or soup pot. Add the onions and fry for 3–4 minutes, stirring frequently, until the onions begin to soften. Add the garlic and chipotle chilli powder, plus some of the adobe sauce, if using. Cook, stirring, for 1 minute, then mix in the corn kernels and cook for another 3 minutes, stirring often.

Pour the chicken stock into the pan, add the salt and pepper, and the chopped corn cobs. Bring to a boil, then reduce the heat under the pan to a simmer and allow to cook for 30 minutes, stirring occasionally.

Meanwhile, when the pepper has charred, remove it from the oven and place in a plastic bag. Twist the bag closed and set the pepper aside for 10 minutes – this will make the skins easier to remove. Peel and deseed the pepper, then dice the flesh. Place in a blender with 125ml (½ cup) cream for the garnish and purée thoroughly. Pour the mixture through a chinois or fine sieve and transfer the sauce to a squeezy bottle with a nozzle.

Remove the soup from the heat and discard the corn cobs. Allow to cool briefly, then purée the soup in batches in a blender until very smooth. Pour the puréed soup through a chinois or fine sieve to remove any traces of the skins of the corn kernels, then return the soup to the saucepan.

Add the remaining 125 ml (½ cup) of cream to the soup and allow to heat through gently for 10–15 minutes, stirring occasionally. Adjust the seasoning to taste, stirring in more of the adobe sauce, if using, as desired to achieve a spicier flavour.

Divide the soup among serving bowls and squirt or drizzle the red pepper cream sauce attractively over the surface to garnish. Serve hot.

Cuisinart food processor to help grind the piñons until they are fine and starting to exude oil. She calls this the 'butter' stage. The nuts are then blended with cornmeal and melted semi-sweet chocolate. Egg yolks, sugar and vanilla (another ingredient native to Mexico) are whisked together and incorporated into the chocolate piñon mixture to give a surprisingly solid batter that simply needs to be pressed into the cake tin.

'This recipe uses European chocolate,' Lois admits, 'because it gives a better result. The indigenous style of chocolate was for moles and drinks and it's just not as good in desserts. Pastry chefs would turn over trying to use that stuff.'

She is keen for everyone to put on an apron and join her at the demonstration bench, to have a go at preparing ingredients and sampling each dish as it comes together. Sadly, this is a fairly unusual occurrence. 'You people are so lucky,' she says to our small class of six. 'Normally we have 30 people in here and it is difficult to pass everything around.'

She is sensitive to each participant's fondness for spicy foods, and prepares mild and medium-hot versions of the corn soup, handing round an extra serving of chipotles in adobo sauce at serving time for those who want to crank the heat level up even further. Chipotles are smoked jalapeño chillies with a wonderfully

savoury, meaty and piquant flavour. 'Don't bother trying to smoke your own chipotle chillies at home,' Lois advises. 'The Oaxacans have already perfected it.'

She does explain, however, how to make dried chipotle chilli powder by grinding a whole dried chipotle in a spice mill. 'You could take the seeds out first if you wanted a milder flavour, or leave them in for more heat. In fact I know a man who just grinds the seeds.'

Her main course is a dish of roast quail stuffed with a mixture of breadcrumbs, corn kernels, the local black walnuts, chives and sage. The accompanying sauce features squawberries, an indigenous

OPPOSITE: ADOBE BUILDINGS ARE THE NORM IN OLD SANTE FE, AND ARE NOT ALLOWED TO REACH MORE THAN FOUR STOREYS HIGH.

RIGHT: CHILLI RISTRA HANGING OUTSIDE AN ADOBE HOUSE.

spice. For those who would struggle to purchase or grow these at home, Lois demonstrates how to use pink peppercorns as a substitute. 'Pink peppercorns do not taste as tart as squawberries,' she says, 'but adding a teaspoon of freshly squeezed lemon juice keeps the flavour tart.'

Most of the students are thirty- and forty-somethings on holiday in the area. After lunch, they are keen to get Lois to sign a copy of her award-winning book, and purchase food and equipment from the well-stocked store at the entrance to the school. The small cast-iron mesh grill designed to dry-roast and char chillies, bell peppers, tomatoes, garlic and onions over a regular gas or electric stovetop burner is particularly coveted. The molcajete, or three-legged traditional lava stone mortar from Mexico, is ideal for making guacamole — not so great for the airlines' new luggage allowances.

Also in New Mexico
Tex-Mex expert and food personality Jane Butel offers hands-on and demonstration classes at her school in Albuquerque, New Mexico. Visit www.janebutel.com for details.

Courses currently available

Cuisines of Mexico I, II, III & IV — Includes recipes such as Shrimp Cocktail with Avocado and Chipotle Chiles, Vera Cruz Style Fish, Rice Tumbado and Cream Cheese Pie with Pineapples.

Fajitas — Complete instruction and demonstration of the menu including Marinated Steak Fajitas, Chunky Avocado Salsa, Roasted Tomatillo Salsa, Habañero Pickled Onions, and Jicama and Orange Salad with Red Chile Vinaigrette Dressing.

All classes last about 2 hours 30 minutes. No accommodatioon included.

Contact: Sante Fe School of Cooking
Upper Level
Plaza Mercado
116 West San Francisco Street
Sante Fe
New Mexico 87501
Tel +1 505 983 4511
Fax +1 505 983 7540
www.santafeschoolofcooking.com

Woodstock Inn Chef for a Day, Vermont, USA

The saying goes 'if you can't get stand the heat, get out of the kitchen', but here is a chance to test whether you *can* stand the heat, working side by side with the chefs at one of America's most prestigious country resorts. Woodstock (no, not that one) may appear to be a sleepy ol' town in the Vermont backwoods, but during the on-season, golfers, skiiers, snowboarders, hunters, hikers, cyclists, equestrians, canoeists and fishing enthusiasts, as well as honeymooners and weekenders, descend on the area, and all that fresh air and healthy activity makes for hungry customers. Woodstock Inn, the area's oldest, caters to them via a fine dining restaurant, casual café-cum-bistro and a tavern, in a sprawling yet cosy white wood building with shuttered windows evocative of yesteryear. They'd love you to come stay, but are happy to put you to work too.

It's like the fires of hell, or so one imagines, when chef Ed Robinson lifts a cover from the massive old-fashioned industrial cooking range in the kitchen of the Woodstock Inn. Vermont, so the theory goes, is too cold to be bothered with air conditioning. Well, baby, it may be cold outside, but it's %&@£*!!! hot in here. So hot that wearing a thick long sleeved jacket and trousers is merciful, because it shields the skin from the intensity of the blazing stove.

'You'll get used to it – want some more water?' says chef de partie Jarred Seega. 'The average temperature in the kitchen in summer is 49-54°C (120–130°F). I lose about 9 kg (20 lb) every summer, but you're so busy you don't really think about it. It's almost part of the passion, part of the job. However we do have to make sure the interns don't focus on the heat too much of the time, otherwise they don't get the job done.'

Jarred began his cheffing career as a Chef for a Day at the Woodstock Inn, so this taster programme is as much for the could-bes as the wannabes and pure fantasists. Limited to two participants at a time, the course is not a full day but an afternoon session, from 2pm until

around 5pm, followed by dinner in Woodstock Inn's elegant dining room. It starts with pulling on the professional chefs' white uniform, and taking a tour of the two floors of kitchens, store rooms and other catering support facilities. Then there is a session in the baking and pastry section, perhaps preparing a selection of chocolates and petits four, before moving upstairs to the main kitchen.

It's very much like a home kitchen, yet nothing like it at all. The big stoves and ovens you expect, but not the bank of steam baths stretching alongside. These

OPPOSITE: REMOTENESS IS A LARGE PART OF THE APPEAL OF VERMONT'S BACKWOODS.

RIGHT: THE REGION IS ESPECIALLY PROUD OF ITS PURE MAPLE SYRUP.

New England Lobster and Crab Cakes with Spicy Remoulade

MAKES 10

1 tablespoon extra virgin olive oil

2 tablespoons finely chopped yellow bell
pepper

2 tablespoons finely chopped red bell
pepper

2 tablespoons finely chopped red onion

1 teaspoon chopped garlic

250 g (8 oz) lobster meat

250 g (8 oz) lump crab meat

2 tablespoons chopped capers

60 g (2½ oz) (1 cup) fresh breadcrumbs,
plus extra for coating

225 g (7½ oz) (1 cup) mayonnaise

2 tablespoons lemon juice

a few drops of Worcestershire
sauce

a few drops of Tabasco sauce

salt and freshly ground black pepper

about 2–3 tablespoons clarified butter

FOR THE SPICY REMOULADE

100 g (3½ oz) (½ cup) mayonnaise

1 tablespoon finely diced yellow bell
pepper

1 tablespoon finely diced red bell pepper

1 tablespoon finely chopped red onion

1 teaspoon crushed (minced) garlic

2 tablespoons chopped cornichons

1 tablespoon chopped capers

1 tablespoon lemon juice

a little cayenne pepper

a few drops of Tabasco sauce

salt and freshly ground black pepper

Frying with clarified butter gives a buttery taste yet allows these shellfish cakes to cook at a higher temperature than they could if regular butter were used. This results in a crisper finish, and less fumes in the kitchen. At the Woodstock Inn, this dish is served with a coleslaw made from green cabbage, carrot, and yellow and red bell peppers, plus corn kernels that they smoke themselves over apple wood chips.

Heat the olive oil in a frying pan. Add the yellow and red bell peppers, red onion and garlic and sauté lightly.

In a large mixing bowl, place the lobster and crab meat. Add the sautéed vegetables and capers, then the fresh breadcrumbs, and carefully mix by hand so as not to break up the pieces of lobster and crab meat.

When the ingredients are well combined, carefully add the mayonnaise and enough lemon juice to give a firm but moist consistency that will hold its shape when sautéed. Season the mixture to taste with Worcestershire sauce, Tabasco sauce, salt and pepper.

Divide the mixture into 10 cakes, which will weigh about 75 g (3 oz) each.

Place the additional fresh breadcrumbs in a wide low-sided dish and add the cakes one by one, turning them to coat lightly and evenly with the breadcrumbs. Transfer to a baking sheet covered with parchment paper and place in the fridge to chill for at least 30 minutes. This will help the cakes to hold their shape when you are frying them.

Meanwhile, to make the remoulade, combine the first eight ingredients in a mixing bowl and stir until thoroughly combined. Season the mixture to taste with cayenne, Tabasco sauce, salt and pepper — it should have a kick.

Heat the clarified butter in a wide frying pan or skillet and fry the cakes in small batches until golden brown on each side. Transfer the cooked cakes to a baking tray lined with paper towel to drain and place in a warm low oven to keep hot while you cook the remainder.

RIGHT: AT WORK IN THE INN'S BAKEHOUSE.

FAR RIGHT: A CHOCOLATE CAKE FROM THE FINE DINING
RESTAURANT WITH ICE CREAM FROM WORLD-FAMOUS
LOCAL SUPPLIERS BEN AND JERRY.

are for holding the cooked components of a dish ready for service. Make polenta at home and, even if you keep it in a warm place, it will start to firm up and form a crust. Here the cooked cornmeal porridge flavoured with cream and butter is transferred to a white plastic tub, covered and kept in hot water, ready to serve alongside herb-crusted rack of lamb, local Green Mountain blue cheese, shoestring potatoes and basil demi-glace.

The risotto is substantially different to that made at home. In the professional kitchen it's stirred to ensure stray grains of rice are easily removed from the sides of the pan and all the grains cook evenly. The stock, at least for the dish of Maine lobster risotto with butternut squash, asparagus and morels, is not stock or even broth but boiling salty water. 'We wanted a neutral flavour for this particular dish because of the delicately flavoured vegetables,' Ed explains. 'Chicken or veal broth would over-flavour it.'

When the rice is 90 per cent cooked, the mixture is taken from the pot and spread evenly over a large baking tray lined with parchment paper to cool it quickly. Another sheet of parchment is placed on top, to prevent the risotto from drying out, and weighted down with teaspoons, so that the paper doesn't curl up.

'Then, to order, we add the vegetables, cream and a touch of butter, and return it to the boil to finish it,' says Ed. The almost-cooked rice mixture tastes surprisingly salty. 'Remember, though, that once the vegetables are added, the salt will be seasoning them too.'

ALTHOUGH SPACIOUS AND LEAFY, THE WOODSTOCK INN
IS IN THE HEART OF THE SMALL TOWN OF WOODSTOCK.

Ed spends the afternoon switching between various side dishes, from spaetzli, to polenta, to turkey stuffing, and back to the risotto, never measuring anything, never letting things burn or overcook, naturally laid-back. Still even he is irritated by the number of spaetzli clumps he has to discard. 'It's not that they taste bad, they just don't look very good.' There's another difference between home and professional kitchens: in real life, you'd eat the ugly spaetzli.

Once Ed has finished simmering — not boiling — the Yukon Gold potatoes, Jarred takes charge of the mash. He puts the spuds through a vegetable mill, adds warm milk and butter melted together, and combines them in a large Hobert mixer to produce a very smooth mashed potato. 'Once you've cooked the potatoes, it's important to drain and mash them quickly, otherwise they're over,' says Jarred. 'We don't measure the ingredients we add to the mash, we go by taste.' Texture, however, is clearly a key indicator of doneness used constantly by both chefs as well. When done, he uses a frying pan to scoop the mash from the gigantic mixing bowl into the stainless steel tray that will hold it in the steam bath until service.

Concluding the kitchen session, the guest 'chefs' are taken to the waitstaff briefing held before the dining room opens to customers each evening. The waiters and hosts know the restaurant's signature dishes well already, but need to be given details of the soup of the day, the *amuse*

bouche the chefs devised that afternoon, and what dishes are on the prix fixe menu. It's not enough just to be able to give diners the name of the day's soup, they need to be able to convey specifics such as whether it's creamy or suitable for vegetarians.

Similarly, the front-of-house staff keep the chefs up-to-date on all the changes in the numbers of advance table bookings, so they are able to gauge exactly how much of each menu component needs to be prepared in advance. 'It's a balancing act,' says Jarred. 'We don't want to do too little because we don't want to tell the customer we don't have something, but we don't want to make too much either because then it could go to waste.'

Frugality is an important trait of any food business, even when it caters to the luxury market. Here, leftover brownies may be used to make truffles, while bread is turned into turkey stuffing. It's just one of the secrets of success in the trade that becomes more significant when you have the chance to be a real chef for a day.

Other chef-style courses

Working in conjunction with top-name chefs in various countries, L'Ecole des Chefs Relais & Châteaux offers a stage programme for the enthusiastic amateur and emerging chef. Visit www.ecoledeschefs.com for details.

NATIVE AMERICAN INGREDIENTS SUCH AS PUMPKIN AND CORN ARE USED TO GOOD EFFECT ON THE WOODSTOCK INN'S MENUS.

This cookery course is currently the only course offered by the Woodstock Inn. Accommodation is included.

Contact: Woodstock Inn and Resort
14 The Green
Woodstock
Vermont 05091
Tel +1 917 441 2313
Fax +1 802 457 6699
www.woodstockinn.com

Index

Acknowledgments

The publisher would like to thank the following photographers, agencies and organisations for their kind permission to reproduce the photographs in this book:

4 Pia van Spaendonck
6 Jason Lowe
8 Richard L'Anson/Lonely Planet Images
10–12 Peter Mack
13 left Greg Elms/Lonely Planet Images
13 right Richard l'Anson/Lonely Planet Images
14 James Davis Travel Photography
17–18 Sydney Seafood School
19 Geoff Lung
20 Eric Meola/Getty Images
23–24 Stephen Elphick/Wine Country Cooking School
25 Jon Hicks/Corbis
26 Michael S. Yamashita/Corbis
27 courtesy of Aldeburgh Cookery School
29 left William Shaw/Country Living/
    National Magazine Company/Retna UK
29 right William Shaw/Country Living/
    National Magazine Company/Retna UK
30 left Pippa Lain/Suffolk Skies Partnership
30 right David Kirkham/Suffolk Skies Partnership
31 Jason Lowe/Food & Travel Magazine
32–37 Bettys & Taylors of Harrogate
38 Preston Schlebusch
40–41 Roger Stayte Photography/ Walnut Grove
    Cookery School
43 Chris Hellier/Corbis
44 Adrian Greeman/Aspect Picture Library
46–47 Food Lover's Tour of Paris
48–49 Richard Turpin/Aspect Picture Library
50 Chris Coe/Axiom Photographic Agency
51–54 Pineapple PR
55 left Christian Sarramon
55 right Christian Sarramon
56–57 Zoe Hatziyannaki
58 & 60 Kieran Scott/Cuisine Magazine
61 James Davis Travel Photography

62 Jill Mead/Axiom Photographic Agency

63 Taj Hotel, Resorts & Palaces

64 Sonia Lakshman/On the go

65 Arjun Vama/On the go

66 Charles Coates/Impact

67 left Teresa Hayhurst/Food & Travel Magazine

67 right Sonia Lakshman/On the go

68 & 70 Peter Cassidy

71 Kevin Dunne/courtesy of Ballymaloe Cookery School

72 Tim Allen/courtesy of BallymaloeCookery School

73 Peter Cassidy

74 Joe Beynon/Axiom Photographic Agency

76 Diane Seed's Roman Kitchen

77 Angela lo Priore/Diane Seed's Roman Kitchen

78 Renzo Frontoni/Axiom Photographic Agency

79 Peter M Wilson/Axiom Photographic Agency

80 Ellen Rooney/Axiom Photographic Agency

81 Philippe Hochart/The Coselli School of
    Tuscan Cuisine

82–83 Marco Guido Cardelli/The Coselli School of
    Tuscan Cuisine

84–85 Philippe Hochart/The Coselli School of
    Tuscan Cuisine

86 Ellen Rooney/Axiom Photographic Agency

88 left Geoff Lung

88 right Sara Cossiga/Venice and Veneto Gourmet

90 Christian Sarramon

91 Dario Pinton/Venice and Veneto Gourmet

92 Mikkel Vang

93–95 Craig Holloway/Kimberley Lodge Cookery School

96 Nik Wheeler/Corbis

97 Craig Holloway/Kimberley Lodge Cookery School

98 Ken Graham/Impact

100 Stephen Kearney/Nick Nairn Cook School

102 Gareth Morgans/BBC Worldwide 2002/Nick Nairn
    Cook School

103 Stephen Kearney/Nick Nairn Cook School

104 Glenn Beanland/Lonely Planet Images

106 Raffles Culinary Academy

107 Geoff Lung

108 Raffles Culinary Academy

109 left Geoff Lung

109 right Andy Johnstone/Impact

110 John Lawrence/The Travel Library

112 Peter Cassidy

114–115 J.Sparshatt

116 Georg Wright/Axiom Photographic Agency

118 Roger Davies

119 Peter Cassidy

120 Ian George/Travel Ink

121 Lisa Linder

122 Alex Brandell/Malmo Tourism

124 Jan-Erick Andersson/Malmo Tourism

126 Alex Brandell/Malmo Tourism

127 left Jan-Erick Andersson/Malmo Tourism

127 right Patrick Tragardh/Malmo Tourism

128 Jeremy Horner/Panos Pictures

129 & 131 The Oriental, Bangkok

132 Geoff Lung

133 John Hay/Lonely Planet Images

134 Macduff Everton/Corbis

135–139 Four Seasons Resort, Chiang Mai

140 Culinary Institute of America/On location

143–145 Culinary Institute of America

146 James Davis Travel Photography

147 Robert Wartell/Inn on the Alameda

148 John Hay/Lonely Planet Images

150 Eddie Brady/Lonely Planet Images

151 Ralph Lee Hopkins/Lonely Planet Images

152 Chris Coe/Axiom Photographic Agency

153 Dave Bartruff/Corbis

155–156 Woodstock Inn & Resort

157 left Jenny Acheson/Axiom Photographic Agency

157 right Chris Coe/Axiom Photographic Agency

Every effort has been made to trace the copyright
holders for photographs. We apologise in advance
for an unintentional omission and would be pleased
to insert the appropriate acknowledgement in any
subsequent edition.